IPAD 10TH

USER GUIDE

A Simplified Manual With Complete Step By Step Instructions For Beginners & Seniors On How To Operate The iPad 10th Generation Like A Pro With iPadOS Tips And Tricks

BY

TERRY HARLEY

Table of Contents

INTRODUCTION

The new iPad 10 released in October 2022 features the A14 Bionic chip, thinner bezels, a USB-C port, a bigger screen & more, and its price starts at $449.

The iPad 10th gen is available in yellow, silver, pink, & blue colour options.

FEATURES OF IPAD 10TH GENERATION

Design

Apple updated the low-cost iPad's design with the release of the 10th-gen model, introducing a new design that looks like the iPad Air & iPad Pro.

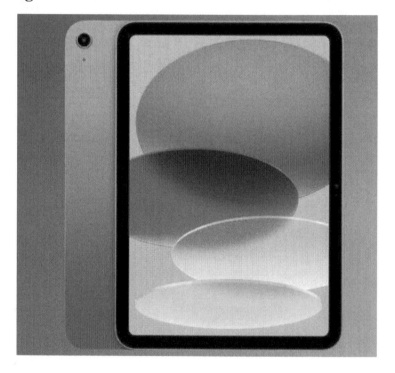

The new iPad has an aluminum chassis with subtle bezels and smooth, rounded edges similar to the iPad Air. It's available in 4 colours, which include yellow, silver, pink, & blue.

The iPad is 248.6mm long, 179.5mm wide, 7mm thick, & weighs 477g.

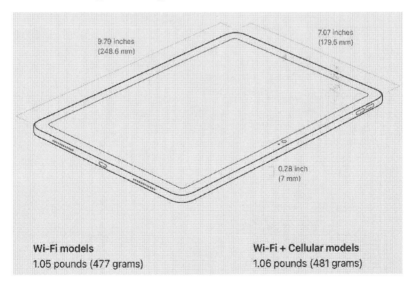

Even with an all-screen design, the iPad doesn't use Face ID. It has a fingerprint recognition sensor built into the power button which allows it to use Touch ID to unlock your iPad, gain access to applications, authenticate purchases, etc.

The new iPad makes use of USB-C for the 1st time, with Apple moving away from Lightning on all iPad models.

Screen

The new iPad has a 10.9" Retina LED screen with a 2360 by 1640 resolution at 264.0 pixels per inch.

Apple increased the iPad's display size by removing the Home button, but the iPad still features 500 nits of maximum brightness. The new iPad supports True Tone, which allows it to adjust the display's colour & intensity to match the lighting around you.

RAM

The iPad has 4 GB RAM.

Storage

The device is available in 64 GB & 256 GB size options.

Battery life

The device has a 28.60-watt lithium-polymer battery, which allows it to provide about 10 hours of battery life when browsing the Internet or watching movies.

Rear camera

The new iPad has a 12-megapixel wide-angle camera with an aperture of $f/1.8$, Burst mode, Smart HDR 3.0 support, Live Pictures, automatic photo stabilization, etc.

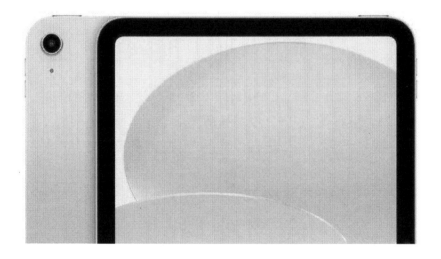

The iPad also has a 12MP Ultra Wide-angle front camera with a view field of 122-degree & an aperture of f/2.40

CHAPTER 1

DEVICE SETUP

→ Long-press the Top button to switch on your tablet.

→ "Hello" will be shown on your screen in different languages. Adhere to the directives on your display to begin set up.

→ Choose one of the languages.

➔ Pick a country or region.
➔ Check out the Quick-Start request. Click on the **Setup Manually** option to manually setup your iPad.

➔ Connect to a WiFi network from the list, or use a Cellular connection to activate & continue your device configuration.

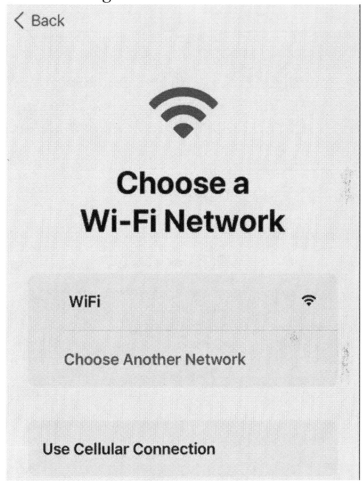

➔ Go through the Privacy Info, and then touch the **Continue** or the **Learn More** button.
➔ Touch the **Continue** button, and then adhere to the directives on your screen to setup the Touch

ID feature, or touch the **Setup Later** button to jump this step.

➔ Type a code & re -enter the code to confirm.

➔ You can decide to setup your tablet as a new one, move your data from an android device or restore it from a back-up. Select the option you like and then adhere to the guideline on your display. If there's no available back up, tap on the **Don't Transfer Applications & Data** option.

Apps & Data

Choose how you want to transfer apps and data to this iPI

Restore from iCloud Backup	>
Restore from Mac or PC	>
Transfer Directly from iPhone	>
Move Data from Android	>
Don't Transfer Apps & Data	>

➔ Type your Apple ID details, and then select Next. Or you can click on the **Forgot your**

password or don't have an Apple ID? Option if you do not have an Apple ID and adhere to the guidelines on your screen.

< Back   Next

Apple ID

Sign in with your Apple ID to use iCloud, the App Store, and other Apple services.

Apple ID	j.appleseed@icloud.com
Password	Required

Forgot password or don't have an Apple ID?

Your Apple ID information is used to enable Apple services when you sign in, including iCloud Backup which automatically backs up the data on your device in case you need to replace or restore it. Your device serial number may be used to check eligibility for service offers. See how your data is managed...

Use different Apple IDs for iCloud & other

→ Go through the terms and condition and then agree to them.

→ Checkout the Make this your iPad screen. Adhere to the directions on your screen to install the desired apps or features.

→ Go through the Improve Siri and Dictation, Keep your iPad Up to Date, and Screen Time prompts, and then click on Continue & adhere to the directions on your screen to set it up or click on the Setup Later button.

→ Go through the iPad Analytic prompt & click on the Continue button.

→ Go through the Applications Analytic prompt and then click on the **Share with Application Developer** option or the **Do not Share** option.

→ Choose your screen **appearance**, then touch the **Continue** button.

→ Click on **Get Started** to start making use of your device.

CHAPTER 2

FUNDAMENTALS

Wake your tablet

Your device turns off the screen to save power, locks & sleep when not in use.

To wake your device carry out any of the below:

→ Press the button at the top of your device.

→ Tap your iPad's screen.

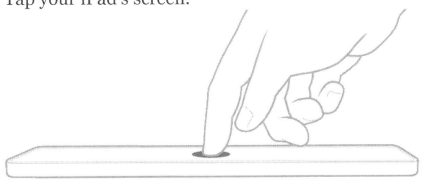

Unlock your device with Touch ID

If you enabled Touch ID when setting up your device, simply place the finger you registered with Touch ID on the button at the top of your device to unlock your iPad.

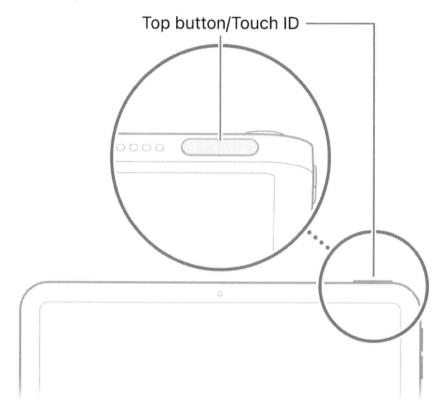

Top button/Touch ID

Press the button at the top of your iPad to lock it again. Your iPad will lock automatically if you do not tap the screen for about a minute.

Unlock your device with a passcode

If you created a passcode when setting up your device, adhere to the directives below to unlock your device with the passcode:

➔ Swipe up from the lower part of your iPad's Lock Screen.

➔ Type the passcode you created to unlock your device.

Learn iPad gestures

Use the following gestures to control your device.

➔ **Tap/Touch.** Use any of your fingers to touch an item on your iPad's screen briefly.

➔ **Long-press/touch & hold.** Long-touch an item on your display till something happens.

➔ **Swipe.** Move one of your fingers across your display quickly.

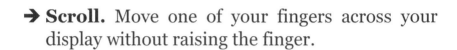

→ **Scroll.** Move one of your fingers across your display without raising the finger.

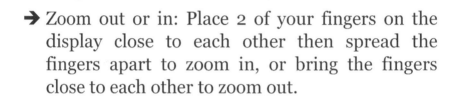

→ Zoom out or in: Place 2 of your fingers on the display close to each other then spread the fingers apart to zoom in, or bring the fingers close to each other to zoom out.

→ **Return to the Home Screen.** Swipe up from the lower edge of your display to go back to your iPad's Home Screen from any application.

➔ **Controls Centre.** Swipe down from the upper right edge of your display to reveal the Controls Centre; Long-press one of the controls to view more options

➔ **Access the Application Switcher.** Use one of your fingers to swipe up from the lower edge, stop in the middle of your iPad's display, and then raise your finger. Swipe to the right to view open applications, then touch the application you would like to make use of.

➔ **Switch between open applications.** Swipe to the right or left along the lower edge of your iPad's display to move from one open application to another.

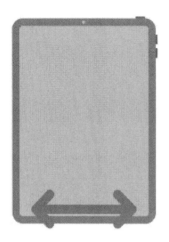

→ **Open the Dock in the application.** Swipe up from the lower edge of your iPad's display and pause to bring out the Dock. To quickly launch another application, simply touch the application's icon in the Dock.

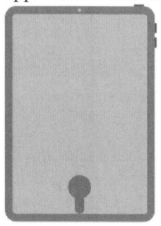

→ **Use Siri.** Say "Hey Siri." Or long-press the button at the top of your tablet while making your request. Then Release the button.

→ **Switch off your device.** At the same time, long-press your iPad's top button & one of the Volume buttons till you see the sliders, then slide the power off slider. Or enter the Settings application, touch General, then touch Shut Down.

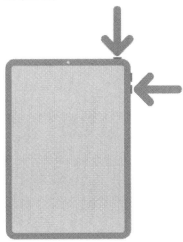

Find the Settings application on your device

In the Settings application, you can look for the iPad settings you want to adjust, like ringtone, password, etc.

➔ On your iPad's Home Screen, touch the Settings app's icon to open the Settings application

Tap Settings to change iPad settings (volume, screen brightness, and more).

➔ To bring out the search field, simply swipe down from the upper part of your display, type a word—iCloud, for instance—then touch one of the settings on the left part of your display.

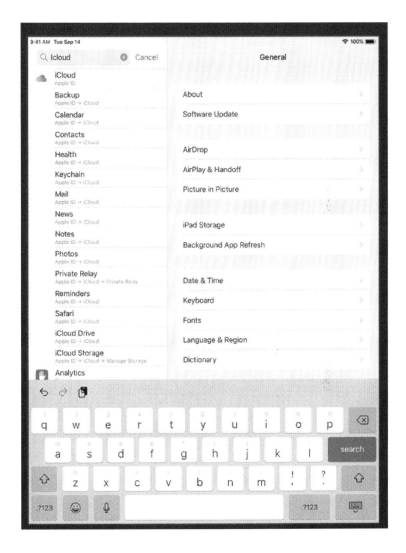

Install a physical SIM

You can insert a nano-SIM in your iPad.

➜ Put an ejection tool inside the hole on your SIM card tray, then push it into your tablet to release the SIM tray.

➜ Remove the SIM plate from your tablet.
➜ Put the SIM card in the SIM plate properly.

➜ Place the plate inside your device.
➜ If your SIM card has a PIN, carefully insert the PIN when asked to.

Manage your mobile data service

➜ Enter the Settings application, and touch Cellular Data.
➜ Carry out any of the below:
  ➢ Limit all data to Wi-Fi: Deactivate Cellular Data.
  ➢ Activate or deactivate LTE & roaming: Touch Cellular Data Options.
  ➢ Activate Personal Hotspot: Touch the **Setup Personal Hotspot** button, and then adhere to the directives on your display.
  ➢ Manage your mobile account: Touch Carrier Service or Manage [Name of Account].

Connect your iPad to the Internet

You can use a WiFi network or your iPad's mobile network to connect your device to the internet.

Connect your iPad to Wi-Fi

➜ Enter the Settings application, touch Wi-Fi, and then activate Wi-Fi.
➜ Click on any of the below:
  ➢ A WiFi network: Type the access code, if necessary.

> ➢ Others: Join a private network. Type the private network name, security type, & password.

If the Wi-Fi icon 📶 appears at the upper part of your display, it means that your device has connected to a WiFi network.

Join a Personal Hotspot

If another iPad or an iPhone shares a Personal Hotspot, you can make use of its mobile Internet connection.

→ Launch the Settings application, touch WiFi, and then select the name of the iPad or iPhone that's sharing the Personal Hotspot.
→ If prompted for a passcode on your iPad, insert the passcode specified in the Settings application> Cellular > Personal Hotspot on the device that's sharing the Personal Hotspot.

Connect your tablet to a mobile network (WiFi + Cellular version)

If your device doesn't have a Wi-Fi network, it will automatically connect to the mobile data network of your carrier. If your device does not connect, check the below:

→ Make sure your SIM card is unlocked & activated.
→ Navigate the Settings application, and touch Cellular Data.
→ Make sure cellular data is enabled.

Manage your Apple ID settings on your iPad

An Apple ID is an account that can be used to access Apple services such as iTunes Store, Application Store, Face-Time, Apple Music, iCloud, etc.

Log in with your Apple ID

If you did not login when setting up your device, adhere to the guideline below:

→ Launch the settings application.
→ Touch the **Sign in to your iPad** button.
→ Type your Apple ID & login code in the appropriate boxes
   You can create an Apple ID if you do not already have one.
→ If your account is protected with two-factor authentication, simply type the 6-digit verification code.

Change your Apple ID settings

→ Launch the Settings application and then touch [your name].
→ Carry out any of the below:
  ➢ Update your profile
  ➢ Use a different password
  ➢ Check out & manage your subscription
  ➢ Change your billing address or your payment methods
  ➢ And more

Use iCloud on your device

iCloud stores your backups, documents, videos, pictures, etc., and automatically keeps your files updated across all your devices. iCloud gives you one e-mail account & 5GB of free storage.

Change your iCloud settings

Login with your Apple ID, and then adhere to the directives below:

→ Head over to the Settings application, touch [your name], and then touch iCloud.

→ Carry out any of the below:
  ➢ Check your iCloud storage space.
  ➢ Activate the features you would like to use, like iCloud Back up, iCloud Drive, & Photos.

Upgrade, change or cancel your iCloud+ subscription

→ Navigate to the Settings application, touch [your name], then touch iCloud.
→ Touch the **Manage Account Storage,** touch the **Change Storage plan** button, choose one of the options, and then adhere to the directives on your screen.

Page | 27

Show iPad battery percentage

You can see how much battery is left on your device in the status bar.

Enter the Settings application, touch Battery, and then activate Battery Percentage.

Adjust your iPad's volume

Press the volume buttons on your device to increase or reduce your iPad's volume level

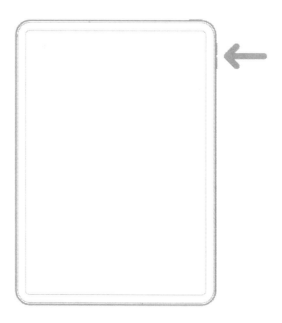

Adjust your iPad's volume in the Control Centre

You can change the volume level in the Controls Centre when your iPad is locked or when you are making use of an application.

Open the Controls Centre and drag the volume slider 🔊.

Mute the sound

Long-press the Reduce Volume button.

Temporarily silence calls & alerts

Open the Controls Centre, touch the **Focus** button, and then touch the **Do Not Disturb** button.

Launch applications on your iPad

You can launch applications from your iPad's Home Screen.

➔ To enter one of the Home Screen pages, swipe up from the lower edge of your display.

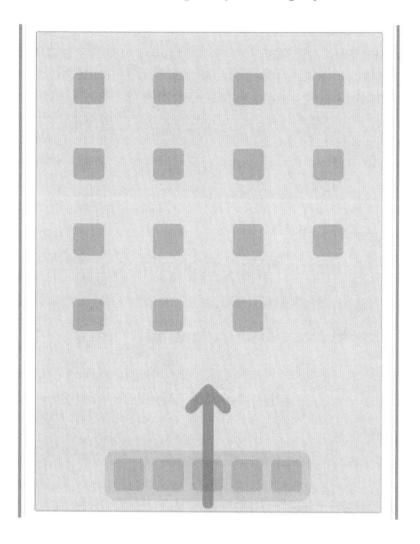

➔ Swipe to the left or right to see applications on the other Home Screen pages.

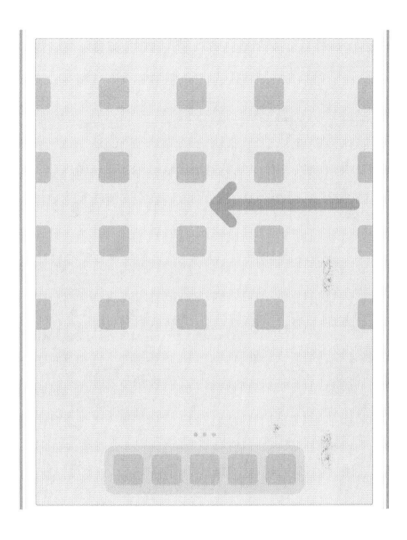

→ Touch an application's icon on your Home screen to launch the application.

→ Swipe up from the lower edge of your display to go back to the Home Screen

Find your applications in the iPad Apps Library

The Applications Library displays your applications arranged into categories like Utilities, Entertainment, Social, etc. Your most used applications are close to the top of your screen and at the top of their category, so you can easily find & launch them.

To Look for an application in the Application Library and open it, simply adhere to the directives below:

➜ From your iPad Home screen, swipe to the left till you pass all the Home Screen pages to access the Applications Library.
You can also quickly enter the Application Library by touching the Apps Library icon  in the Dock at the lower part of your display.

Go to App Library

➜ Touch the Search box at the upper part of your display, and then type the name of the application you are looking for.
Or scroll through the list.
➜ Touch an application's icon to launch it.

Hide & show the Home Screen pages

Since you can find all your applications in the Application Library, you probably don't need a lot of Home screen pages for applications. You can hide some Home screen pages (If you want to see the pages you've hidden, you can simply unhide them.)

➜ Press & hold the Home Screen background till the applications start vibrating.
➜ Touch the dots at the lower part of your display. Next, you will see Thumbnail pictures of your Home Screen pages with checkmarks under them.

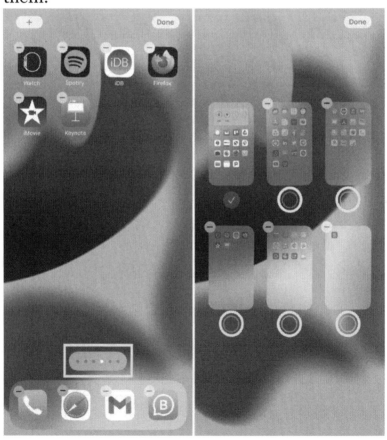

➜ Touch to remove the checkmark under a page to hide the page.
To show the pages you've hidden, just touch to add the check marks

➜ Touch the **Done** button

Tip: To rearrange the Home Screen pages, simply long-press the thumbnail, then drag it to another location, then touch the **Done** button.

Change where new applications get downloaded

When you download a new application from the Apps Store, you can choose to add it to the Apps Library & Home Screen, or just the Apps Library.

➜ Navigate to the Settings application, and touch Home screen & dock.

➜ Select one of the options in the **Newly Downloaded Apps** section.

Move an application from the Apps Library to your Home Screen

You can add an application in the Apps Library to your Home Screen if it isn't already there.

Long-press the application, then touch the **Add to Home Screen** button.

The application will appear on the Apps Library & Home Screen.

Apps Switcher

You can use the Apps Switcher to easily move between apps on your device

→ To check out all your open applications, simply swipe up from the lower edge of your display, then stop in the middle of your screen

→ To see all the open applications, swipe to the right, then touch the application or Split View workspace you would like to use.

Switch between open applications

To move from one open application to another, carry out any of the below:

→ Use a finger to swipe to the left or right along the bottom edge of your display
→ Use 4 or 5 fingers to swipe to the left or right.

Zoom an application to fill your iPad's screen

Some applications for iPhone can be used with iPad, but they may not fill your iPad's big screen. In this situation, touch the Expand icon to zoom in on the application. Touch the Zoom Shrink icon to go back to the original size.

Quit an application

To close an application, open the Apps Switcher, then swipe the application up.

Dictate Text

With Dictation, you can dictate text on your iPad anywhere you can type

Activate Dictation

→ Launch the Settings application, touch General, and tap on Keyboard.
→ Activate the **Enable Dictation** feature.

Dictate text

→ Touch to place the point of insertion where you want to enter text,

→ Touch the Dictate icon 🎤 on your keyboard, then start talking.
As you speak, your device will automatically insert punctuation marks for you when necessary.

→ When you're done, touch the Stop Dictation icon 🎤.

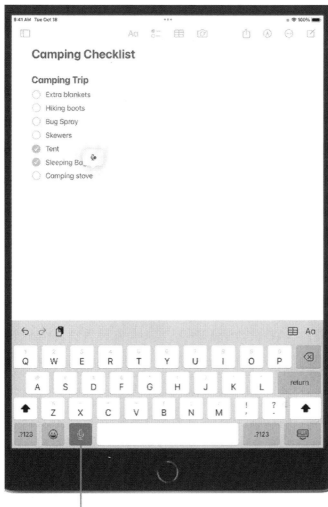

Tap to begin dictation.

Change the on-screen keyboard to a trackpad

➜ Use one of your fingers to long-press the Space bar till the keyboard turns light gray.
➜ Darg around the keyboard to move the point of insertion

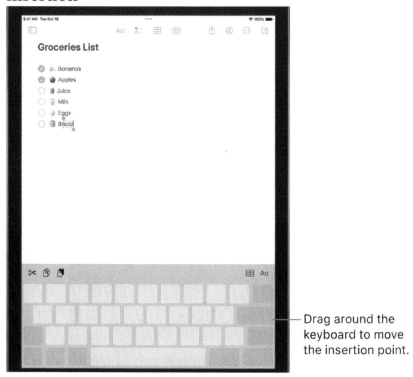

Drag around the keyboard to move the insertion point.

Select, cut, copy, and paste text on iPad

In applications on your device, you can use your keyboard, finger, or Apple Pencil to highlight and edit texts in text fields.

➔ Carry out any of the below to highlight text:

  ➤ Tap a word two times quickly to select the word.

  ➤ Tap a word three times quickly to select the paragraph that the word is in.

  ➤ Highlight a text block: Tap the first word in the block two times quickly and hold the word, then drag to highlight the rest of the block

➔ Once you've selected the text you want to edit, you can type or touch the selection to view the editing options:

- ➢ Touch the **Copy** option to copy the highlighted text.
- ➢ Touch the **Cut** option to cut the highlighted text
- ➢ Paste: Touch the **Paste** option
- ➢ Replace: Check out recommended replacement text.
- ➢ B/I/U: Format the text you've highlighted.
- ➢ The See other options icon

Text replacement

You can create text replacements that you can use to insert a phrase or word by simply typing a few characters. For instance, type "OMW" to insert "On My Way".

➔ To create a text replacement, simply carry out any of the below:

- On-screen keyboard: Long-press the Emoji button😊 or the Switch keyboard key🌐, touch Keyboard settings, and then touch the **Text Replacement** button
- With an external keyboard: Enter the Settings application, touch General, touch Keyboard, and then touch the **Text Replace** button.

➔ Touch the Add button╈ at the upper right part of your display.
➔ Write a phrase in the Phrases box and type the text abbreviation you plan on using in the Shortcut box

Add or remove keyboards for other languages

➔ Enter the Settings application, touch General, and then touch Keyboard
➔ Touch the **Keyboards** button, then carry out any of the below:
- Add keyboard: Touch the **Add a New Keyboard** button, and then select a keyboard. Repeat to add other keyboards.
- Remove a keyboard: Touch the Edit button, click on the Remove icon➖ beside the

keyboard you plan on removing, touch the **Delete** button, and then touch Done.

Switch to another keyboard

Long-press the Emoji button☺ or the Switch keyboard key⊕, then touch the keyboard you want to use.

You can also touch the Emoji button☺ or the Switch keyboard key⊕ to move from one keyboard to another. Keep touching to gain access to other keyboards

Split View

With the Split View feature, you can work with many applications simultaneously on your device. Open 2 applications or 2 windows from the same application, by dividing your screen. For instance, you can launch the Message application & the Maps application at the same time. Or you can open two Safari windows and manage two webpages at the same time.

Open a 2ⁿᵈ application in Split View

➔ While making use of an application, touch the Multitasking Controls icon ••• at the upper part of the application, touch the Split View icon ⊞, then click on the Split View Left icon ▣ to move the current application to the left part of your screen, or the Right Split View button ▣ to move the application to the right.
The application you are making use of will move to one side to create space for your Home Screen

➔ Look for another application on your Home Screen and open it
Both applications will appear in Split View.

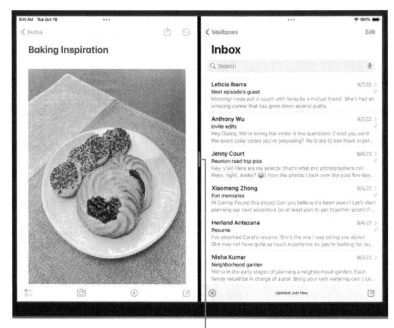

Drag to resize the split.

Replace an application in Split View

If you have 2 applications open in Split View, you can replace any of them with another application.

➔ Swipe down from the Multitasking Controls icon ▦▦▦ at the upper part of the application you want to replace.

The application will drop down, and the other application will move to the side to create space for the Home Screen.

➜ Look for another application on your Home Screen and open it
Both applications will appear in Split View.

Change Split View to Slide Over

If you have 2 windows or applications open in Split View, you can change one of the applications or windows to a Slide Over window — a smaller window that slides in front of the first one.

➜ Touch the Multitasking Controls icon ••• at the upper part of the application or window, then touch the Slide Over icon

Go back to full screen

If you have 2 windows or applications open in Split View, you can remove one of the windows or applications and display the other in full screen. Carry out any of the below:

→ Drag the divider in the middle of the split view to the right or left edge of your display.
→ Touch the Multitasking Controls icon at the upper part of the application you want to display in full screen, then touch the Enter Full Screen icon .

Slide Over

While making use of an application, you can change it to a Slide Over window and open another application behind the Slide Over window. For instance, when making use of the Photos application, you can open the Message application in a Slide Over window and manage the two applications at the same time.

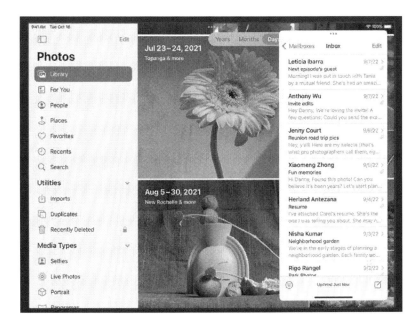

Open an application in Slide Over

➜ While making use of an application, touch the Multitasking Controls icon ••• at the upper part of the application, then touch the Slide Over icon ⬚|

The application will move to the side to create space for the Home Screen

➜ Look for & launch the application you would like to appear behind the Slide Over window.

The 2nd application will open, and the 1st application will appear in a front of it in a Slide Over window.

To open a 3rd application in Slide Over when using Split View, simply swipe up from the lower edge a little bit to reveal the Dock, then drag the 3rd application from the Dock to the Splits View divider.

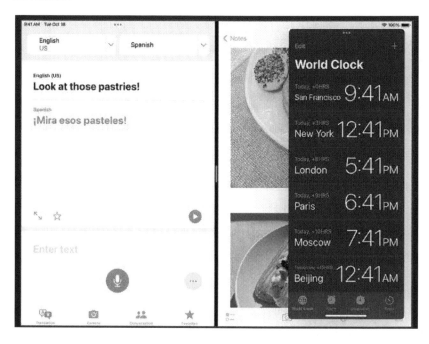

Switch between open applications in Slide Over

➜ Swipe up from the lower edge of the Slide Over window to the middle of your screen, stop, then raise your finger
You will see your entire Slide Over windows
➜ Touch the application you want to use

Page | 50

If you can't find the application, swipe to the right or left through the applications.

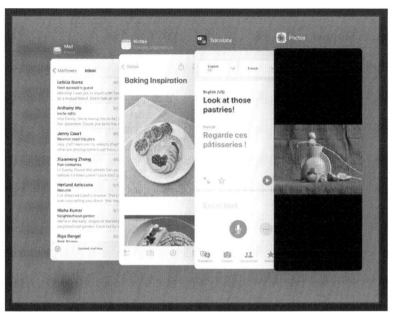

Move the Slide Over window

Carry out any of the below:

→ Drag the Multitasking Controls icon ••• at the upper part of the window to move the window to the other part of your display.

→ Temporarily hide the Slide-Over window: Swipe from the lower edge of the Slide-Over window to the top, or drag a side of the Slide-Over window to the left edge of your display. The window will disappear and a tab will appear to show that the window is still available, simply drag the tab from the left edge of your display to bring the Slide-Over window back to your screen.

Change Slide Over to Split View

Touch the Multitasking Controls icon ▪▪▪ at the upper part of the Slide Over window, touch the Split View icon⬛, then click on the Split View Left icon⬛ to move the current application to the left part of your screen, or the Right Split View button ⬛ to move the application to the right.

Open an item in the middle of your screen

In many applications on your device, such as Message, Files, & Notes, you can open items in the middle of the application window.

➜ Carry out any of the below:
   ➢ Long-press an email in a mailbox in the Mail application
   ➢ Long-press a conversation in the Messages application.
   ➢ Long-press a note in the Notes application
➜ Touch the **Open in a New Window** button. The item will open in the middle of your display, on top of what you are viewing.

You can turn the middle window to full screen by touching the Full Screen button ▨, make the window a Split View window by touching the Split View icon ⬚, or make it a Slide Over window by touching the Slide Over icon ⬚.

Multitask with Picture in Picture mode

With the **Picture in Picture** mode, iPad users can watch a movie or make a FaceTime call while making use of other applications.

While watching a video, touch the Video Shrink button ⬚.

The video window shrinks to one corner of your display to create space for the Home Screen so that you can launch other applications. With the video window showing, you can:

➔ Change the size of the window: Pinch open to increase the size of the window. Pinch closed to reduce the size.
➔ Touch the window to display or hide controls
➔ You can move the window by dragging it to any corner of your display

➜ You can hide the window by dragging it off the right or left edge of your display

➜ Touch the Close icon · to close the window

➜ Touch the Full Screen icon in the small window to go back to full screen

Access features from your Lock Screen

Tuesday, October 18

9:41

The Lock Screen appears when you wake or switch on your device and it displays the date, time, and your latest notifications. Even while your device is locked, you can gain access to info & features you need from your Lock screen.

➔ Swipe to the left to use your iPad's camera.
➔ Swipe down from the upper right corner of your display to gain access to the Control Centre
➔ Swipe up from the middle of your display to view your recent notifications
➔ Swipe to the right to see widgets
➔ Tap your Apple Pencil on your Lock Screen to start writing or drawing in a note. What you create will be stored in the Notes application.

Perform quick actions on your device

In applications, in the Controls Centre, and on your Home Screen, you can previews items, open menus, etc.

➔ In the Photos applications, long-press a photo to preview it and check out an options list.
➔ In the Mail application, long-press an email in a mailbox to preview the contents of the message & view an options list.
➔ On your Home Screen, long-press an app's icon to open the quick action menu. If the icons start

jiggling, touch the **Done** button, and try one more time

➜ Open the Controls Centre, then long-press an item like the brightness control to view more options

Search on iPad

On your iPad, you can search for contacts & applications; you can also check currency & stock info, and more.

➜ Swipe down from the center of your Lock Screen or Home Screen
➜ Type what you want in the search box
➜ Carry out any of the below:
  ➢ Touch the **Search** button to hide the keyboard and show more results
  ➢ Touch a suggested application to open it
  ➢ Perform quick actions: Activate a Focus, run any shortcut, etc.
  ➢ Touch a recommended site to visit it.
  ➢ Get more details about a search recommendation: Touch it, and then touch a search result to open it.
  ➢ Touch the Clear icon⊗ in the search box to begin another search

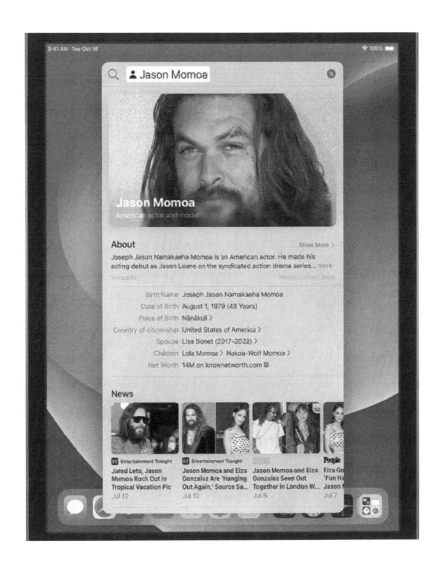

AirDrop

AirDrop allows you to send pictures, locations, sites, videos, etc to other Apple devices that are close to you. AirDrop sends data via Bluetooth & WiFi - both must be enabled.

Send something via AirDrop

→ Open the item, and then touch the AirDrop icon ⬆, the **AirDrop** button, the **Share** button, the More Options icon •••, or any other button that shows the application's sharing options.

→ Click on the AirDrop icon 📶 in the sharing options row, and then select a close-by AirDrop user.

If the individual does not appear as a closeby AirDrop user, tell the person to open the Controls Center on their iOS or iPadOS device and permit AirDrop to receive items. To send to a Mac, tell the Mac user to allow their device to be discovered in AirDrop in the Finder.

Let others send things to you via AirDrop

→ Open the Controls Centre, long-press the upper left set of controls, then touch the AirDrop icon 📶.

→ Touch the **Everyone** option or the **Contact Only** option to choose the individuals you would like to receive items from.

You can choose to accept or reject requests as they arrive.

Take screenshots or screen recordings

You can take a screenshot or record screen activity to share with other people or use in a document.

Take a screenshot

➜ Press & release the Top button & Volume Up button at the same time

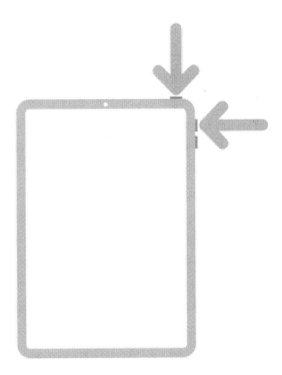

➔ Touch the screenshot's thumbnail in the bottom left edge of your screen, then touch the **Done** button

➔ Touch the **Save to Photos, Save to Files,** or **the Delete Screenshot** button

If you touched the **Save to Photo** option, you can find the screenshot in the Screenshots folder in the Photos application.

Save the full-page screenshot as a PDF file

You can capture a full-page, scrolling screen shot of a website, e-mail, and more that's longer than your iPad's screen length, then save it in PDF format.

➔ Press & release the Top button & Volume Up button at the same time

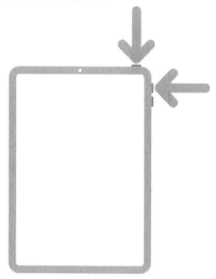

→ Touch the screenshot's thumbnail in the bottom left edge of your screen, then touch the **Full Page** button
→ Carry out any of the below:
  ➤ Save screenshot: Touch the **Done** button, then touch the **Save PDF file to Files,** then select a location, then touch the **Save** button
  ➤ Share screenshot: Touch the Share icon⬆, select one of the sharing options, fill in any needed info, then send the file.

Create a screen recording

You can record your screen & get the audio on your iPad as well.

→ Enter the Settings application, touch Controls Centre, and then touch the Add button⊕ beside Screen Recording.
→ Open the Controls Centre, and click on the Screen Recording button◉.
  Your device will start recording your screen after three seconds.
→ To stop recording, open the Controls Centre, click on the Screen Recording button◉ or the red status bar at the upper part of your display, then touch the **Stop** button.

Enter the Photos application, then open the video.

Draw in applications with the Markup feature

In some applications like Books, Notes, Mail, & Messages, you can annotate pictures, and PDF files, write notes, sketch, etc. using the inbuilt drawing tools.

Show, move & hide the Mark up toolbar

To bring out the Mark-up toolbar in an application that's compatible with Mark-up, touch the Markup icon⒜ or the **Markup** button, then carry out any of the below:

➜ You can move the Mark-up tool bar by dragging it to any edge of your display.
(it's best to drag the toolbar from the middle edge.)

➜ Touch the More icon⊙, then activate Auto-minimize to automatically minimize the toolbar when you are writing or drawing.
Touch the minimized version of the tool bar to display the full toolbar.

➜ Touch the **Done** button or the Hide Markup icon⒜ to hide the toolbar

Draw or write in applications with Mark-up

In the Mark-up tool bar, touch the pencil tool, marker, or pen, then use your Apple Pencil or finger to draw or write.

Carry out any of the below while drawing or writing:

➜ Change the weight of a line: Touch the selected drawing tool in the tool bar, then select one of the options.

➜ Adjust the opacity: Touch the drawing tool you're using in the toolbar, and then slide the slider.

➜ Use a different colour: Select a colour in the Mark-up toolbar

➜ Undo an error: Click on the Reverse icon ↺

➜ Draw a straight line: Touch the ruler in the tool bar, and then draw a line along the ruler's edge.

   ➤ To change the ruler's angle, use 2 fingers to long-press the ruler, then rotate your fingers.

   ➤ You can move the ruler from one place to another by dragging it with 1 finger.

   ➤ Touch the ruler tool in the tool bar once more to hide the ruler

Draw a shape

With the Markup feature, you can draw perfect shapes like circles, clouds, triangles, stars, hearts, arcs, arrows, lines, etc. to use in sketches.

➜ Touch the pencil tool, marker, or pen in the Mark-up toolbar

➜ Use your Apple Pencil or finger to draw a shape in one stroke, then pause

The correct version of the shape will appear and replace what you drew. (If you want to use the free version, click the Reverse button.)

Change your handwritten drawings or text

➔ In the Mark-up panel, select the Lasso tool, then carry out any of the below to highlight the content you want to edit:

- ➢ Tap a drawn object or word two times quickly to select it.
- ➢ Tap a word in a sentence three times to highlight the sentence
- ➢ Highlight a block of text or paragraph: Long-press the 1st word, and drag to the last word. Drag slowly to highlight more accurately.
- ➢ Select multiple drawn objects: Select the Lasso tool, use your Apple Pencil or finger to draw around the object, and then touch the selection.

➔ Once you've selected the content you want to edit, touch it, then carry out any of the below:

- ➢ Duplicate, delete, copy, or cut: Click on one of the options.
- ➢ Move: Long-press the content till it lifts, and then drag it to another location.

Erase an error

In the Mark-up toolbar, touch the eraser tool twice quickly, then carry out any of the below:

→ Pixel Eraser: Select the **Pixel Eraser** option, and then use your Apple Pencil or finger to scrub over the error.
→ Erase an object: Select the **Object Eraser** option, then use your Apple Pencil or finger to tap the object.
→ Switch between object & pixel eraser: Touch the Eraser tool once more, then select the **Object Eraser** option or the **Pixel Eraser** option.

Set sound options

In the Settings application, you can set options for ringtones & alert tones, and alerts & ringer volumes.

→ Enter the Settings application, and touch Sound
→ Slide the slider to choose the volume level for alerts & ringer.
→ Touch Ringtone & other options to set sounds for the alert tones & ringing tones.

Change your iPad's wallpaper

Use an image or one of your pictures as your Home Screen or Lock Screen wallpaper.

➔ Enter the Settings application, touch Wallpaper > Choose New Wallpaper.
➔ Carry out any of the below:
   ➢ Select one of the preset images from the group at the upper part of your display.
   The wallpapers that have the Appearance icon

   ⊙ change their appearance when Dark Mode is activated.
   ➢ Choose any of your personal pictures (touch one of the albums, and then touch the picture).

- ➢ Touch the Parallax Effect icon⬚ to activate Perspective Zoom, which will make your wallpaper look like it's moving when your change your viewing angle.
- ➜ Click on the **Set** button and then select any of the below:
  - ➢ Set Home Screen
  - ➢ Set Lock Screen
  - ➢ Set Both

To activate the Perspective Zoom feature for a wallpaper you have already set, enter the Settings application, touch Wallpaper, touch the Lock screen or Home screen image, and then touch the **Perspective Zoom** button.

Change your screen brightness manually

To increase or reduce the brightness of your screen, carry out any of the below:

- ➜ Open the Controls Centre and then slide the Brightness slider ☀.
- ➜ Head over to the Settings application, touch Display and Brightness, then slide the slider.

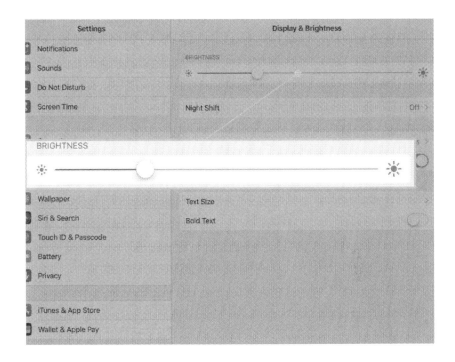

Adjust your screen brightness automatically

Your device uses its inbuilt ambient light sensor to change the screen's brightness to match its current light conditions.

➔ Enter the Settings application, and touch Accessibility.
➔ Touch Display and Text Size, and then activate the **Auto-Brightness** feature.

Enable or disable Dark mode

The Dark Mode setting gives your device a dark colour scheme that is ideal for low-light environments.

Carry out any of the below:

➔ Open the Controls Centre, press & hold the Brightness key☀, and then click on the Appearance button◑ to enable or disable the **Dark Mode** feature.

➔ Enter the Settings application, touch Display and Brightness, and then choose Dark to activate Dark mode or Light to deactivate it.

Set Dark Mode to activate or deactivate automatically

→ Enter the Settings application and touch Display and Brightness.
→ Activate Automatic and then touch Options.
→ Choose **Custom Schedule** or **Sunset to Sunrise**.
If you selected the **Custom Schedule** feature, touch the options to set when you want Dark Mode to automatically activate or deactivate.
If you choose the **Sunset to Sunrise** feature, your device will use the information from your clock and location to determine when it is nighttime for you.

Activate or deactivate Night Shift

The Night Shift feature shifts the colour in your screen to the warmer side of the spectrum and can be helpful when you are in a dark room during the day.

Open the Controls Centre, press & hold the Brightness key , and then click on the Night Shift button .

Set Night Shift to activate or disable automatically

→ Navigate to the Settings application, tap Display & Brightness, and then tap Night shifts.
→ Activate Scheduled.
→ To change the colour balance for Night Shift, move the slider under Colour Temperature to the cooler or warmer end of the spectrum.
→ Touch the **From** button, then choose **Custom Schedule** or **Sunset to Sunrise**.
If you selected the **Custom Schedule** feature, touch the options to set when you want Night Shift to automatically activate or deactivate.
If you choose the **Sunset to Sunrise** feature, your device will use the information from your clock and location to determine when it is nighttime

Activate or deactivate True Tone

The True Tone feature automatically adjusts the display's colour & intensity to match the lighting around you.

Carry out any of the below:

➔ Open the Controls Centre, press & hold the Brightness key ✴, and then click on the True Tone button ✴ to enable or disable the **True Tone** feature.
➔ Enter the Settings application, touch Display and Brightness, and then activate or deactivate True Tone.

Rename your iPad

You can change your iPad's name, which is used by your Computer, your Personal Hotspot, AirDrop, & iCloud.

➔ Navigate to the Settings application, touch General, touch About, and then touch Name.
➔ Click on the Clear Text icon ⊗, type another name, and then touch the **Done** button.

Change the time & date on your device

➔ Navigate to the Settings application, tap General, and then touch Date & Time.
➔ Activate any of the below:

➢ Set Automatically: Your device will get the accurate time over the network & update it for your time zone.
➢ 24-hour Time: Your device will show the hours from 0 - 23.

To change the time & date, deactivate the **Set Automatically** feature, then make an adjustment to the date and time on your device.

Change the region & language on your device

➜ Enter the Settings application, touch General, and then touch Language & Region.
➜ Set the following:
   ➢ Your iPad's language
   ➢ Your preferred form of address
   ➢ The format of your calendar
   ➢ Your region
   ➢ The measurement system
   ➢ The temperature unit
   ➢ Live Text

Organize applications in folders on your device

You can arrange your applications into folders to make it easy to find them on your Home Screen pages.

Create folders

➔ Long-press an application on your Home Screen, and then touch the **Edit Home Screen** button. The applications will start jiggling
➔ Drag an application onto another application to create a folder
➔ To change the name of the folder, long-press it, touch the **Rename** button, then type a name.
If the applications start vibrating, touch the background of your Home Screen & try again
➔ When you are done, touch the **Done** button

To delete a folder, simply drag all the applications from the folder to the Home Screen.

Reset the Home Screen & applications to their original layout

➔ Navigate to the Settings application, touch General, and then touch the **Reset** button
➔ Touch the **Reset Home Screen Layout** option.

All the folders you have created will be erased, and the applications you have downloaded will be arranged in alphabetical order after the applications that came with your device.

Remove applications from your device

You can uninstall applications from your device.

Carry out any of the below:

➔ Remove an application from your Home screen: Press & hold the application on your Home Screen, click on the **Remove Application** button, then touch the **Remove from Home Screen** button to keep the application in the Apps Library or touch the **Delete Application** button to remove the application from your device.

➔ Delete an application from your Home Screen & Apps Library: Press & hold the application in the Apps Library, touch the **Delete Application** button, and then touch the **Delete** button.

Use & personalize the Control Center on your device

The Controls Centre on your device provides quick access to useful controls like DND, volume, brightness, & applications.

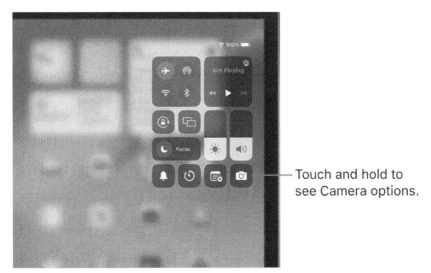

Touch and hold to see Camera options.

To open the Controls Centre, swipe down from the upper right corner of your screen; swipe up from the lower part of your display to close the Controls Centre.

Access more controls in the Control Center

Most controls offer additional options. Press & hold a control to view the available options. For instance, in the Controls Centre, you can:

→ Long-press the upper left set of controls, then touch the AirDrop button to see the AirDrop options.

→ Long-press the Camera button 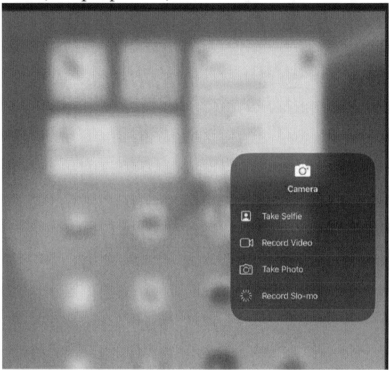 to record a video, snap a picture, etc.

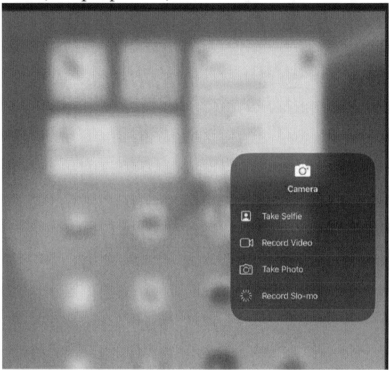

Add & manage controls

→ Enter the Settings application, and then touch Control Center.

→ To remove or add a control, click on the Add button ⊕ or the Remove button ⊖ beside the control.

➔ To change the location of a control, click on the Edit button ≡ beside the control and then drag it to another location.

Change or lock your iPad's screen orientation

Some applications change their view when your iPad is rotated.

You can lock your iPad's screen orientation so that it does not change when your device is rotated.

Open the Controls Centre and then touch the Orientation Lock icon 🔓.

Set an alarm

You can set alarms in the Clock application.

➔ Enter the Clock application, touch Alarm, and then touch the Add icon ✛
➔ Set the time, then select one of the options below:
- Snooze: Give yourself some time to rest
- Sound: Select a ringtone
- Label: Name the alarm
- Repeat: Select when you want the alarm to be activated

➔ Touch the **Save** button.

Touch the **Edit** button, to delete or edit the alarm.

Disable an alarm

Touch the button under the alarm time

Connect Apple Pencil to your device

Remove the Apple Pencil's cover and plug it & a USB-C into the Apple Pencil to USB-C Adapter. Then Plug the other end into your tablet.

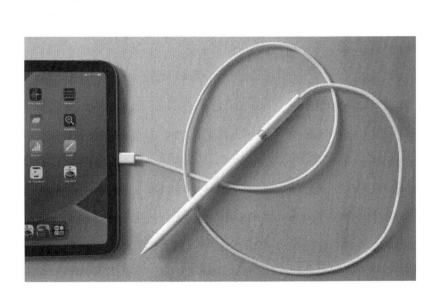

Touch the Pair button when it pops up on your iPad's screen. Wait for the Apple Pencil to connect to your tablet, and then disconnect it from the Adapter.

Don't unplug the Apple Pencil from the Adapter & your iPad if you want your iPad to charge the Apple Pencil

If your Apple Pencil won't connect to your device

→ Remove the Apple Pencil's cover and plug it & a USB-C into the Apple Pencil to USB-C Adapter. Then Plug the other end into your tablet.
→ Restart your tablet, and try pairing once more
→ Enter the Settings application, touch Bluetooth, and ensure Bluetooth is enabled.
→ On that screen, look for your Apple Pencil in the My Devices section. If you see it, click the Details icon ⓘ. Then touch the **Forget this Device** button.
→ Connect your Apple Pencil to your device and touch the **Pair** button when it pops up
→ If you don't see the Pair button, wait for a few minutes while your iPad charges the Apple Pencil. Then try to connect your Apple Pencil once more and wait till you see the Pair button
→ If the Pair button does not pop up, contact apple support.

Handoff

The Handoff feature allows Apple device users to begin something on one Apple device (Mac, Apple Watch, iPad, iPod touch, or iPhone) and continue from where they stopped on another Apple device. For instance, you can start replying to an e-mail on your iPad and finish replying to the e-mail in the Mail application on your MacBook. The Handoff feature supports a lot of Apple applications, such as Safari, Contacts, & Calendar.

Getting started

Before you can use the Handoff feature, make sure of the following:

→ You are using the same Apple ID on the two devices
→ You have activated Handoff, WiFi, & Bluetooth on your MacOS device
(To activate the Handoff feature on MacOS Ventura, simply select Apple menu, select Systems Settings, click on the **General** button in the side bar, click on AirDrop and Handoff on the right part of your display, then activate the **Allow Hand off between Mac & your iCloud device** feature)
(To activate the Handoff feature on macOS 12.50 or before, simply select Apple menu, select Systems Preference, click on the **General** button, then select the **Allow Hand off between Mac & your iCloud device** feature)

→ You have activated Handoff, Bluetooth, & WiFi on your iPad or iPhone
(To activate the Handoff feature, enter the Settings application, touch General, touch AirPlay and Handoff, then activate the Handoff feature)
→ Both devices are in Bluetooth range (about 33ft).

Hand off from another Apple device to your iPad

→ Open your iPad Dock.
→ You will find the application with the Handoff icon on the right end of the Dock, simply touch the application to resume running the application on your device.

Handoff from your iPad to other Apple devices

On other devices, touch or click on the Hand Off icon to resume using the application.

You will find the Handoff icon in the following places on the following Apple devices:

➔ iPhone: At the lower part of the Application Switcher

➔ MacOS devices: The right part of the Dock.

Disable the Handoff feature

➔ iOS or iPadOS devices: Enter the Settings application, touch General, touch AirPlay and Handoff, then disable the Handoff feature

➔ MacOS Ventura: Select Apple menu, select Systems Settings, click on the **General** button in the side bar, click on AirDrop and Handoff on the right part of your display, then deactivate the **Allow Hand off between Mac & your iCloud device** feature.

➔ MacOS 12.50 or before: Select Apple menu, select Systems Preference, click on the **General** button, then unselect the **Allow Hand off between Mac & your iCloud device** feature

Universal Clipboard

The Universal Clipboard allows iPad users to copy or cut content (a picture or text, for instance) on their iPad, and then paste it on another Apple device (Mac, iPad, iPhone, & iPad touch) & vice versa.

Getting started

Before you can use the Universal Clipboard feature, make sure of the following:

→ You are using the same Apple ID on the two devices
→ You have activated Handoff, WiFi, & Bluetooth on your MacOS device
  (To activate the Handoff feature on MacOS Ventura, simply select Apple menu, select Systems Settings, click on the **General** button in the side bar, click on AirDrop and Handoff on the right part of your display, then activate the **Allow Hand off between Mac & your iCloud device** feature)
  (To activate the Handoff feature on macOS 12.50 or before, simply select Apple menu, select Systems Preference, click on the **General**

button, then select the **Allow Hand off between Mac & your iCloud device** feature)

➔ You have activated Handoff, Bluetooth, & WiFi on your iPad or iPhone
(To activate the Handoff feature, enter the Settings application, touch General, touch AirPlay and Handoff, then activate the Handoff feature)

➔ Both devices are in Bluetooth range (about 33ft).

Cut, copy, or paste

➔ Cut: Pinch closed with 3 of your fingers twice
➔ Pinch closed with 3 of your fingers to copy.
➔ Pinch open with 3 of your fingers to paste

You can also long-press a selection, then touch the Paste, Copy, or Cut buttons.

Reset your iPad settings to their defaults

You can return your iPad's settings to their default.

➔ Enter the Settings application, touch General, touch the Transfer or Reset iPad button, and then touch the **Reset** button

➔ Select any of the options
  - Reset All Settings
  - Reset Network Settings
  - Reset Keyboard Dictionary
  - Reset Location and Privacy
  - Reset the Home Screen Layout

Wipe your iPad's data

Erase your device to permanently delete all the data on your device.

➔ Enter the Settings application, touch General, and then touch Transfer or Reset iPad.
➔ Carry out any of below:
  - Prepare your data to transfer to a new iPad: Touch the **Get Started** button, and then adhere to the directives on your display. When you're done, go back to the Settings application, touch General, touch Transfer or Reset iPad, then touch the **Erase All Contents & Setting** button.
  - Erase all data from your iPad: Touch the **Erase All Contents & Setting** button

Use your device as a remote microphone with live listening

You can stream audio from your iPad's microphone to your AirPods or Made For iPad (MFi) hearing aids. This can make it easier for you to hear better in certain situations, for instance, when discussing with someone in a noisy place.

→ If you use AirPods, put them in your ears. If the AirPod does not connect to your iPad automatically, touch the Playback Destination button in the Controls Centre or on your lock screen, and then select your AirPods.

→ To activate or deactivate the **Listen Live** feature, open the Controls Centre, touch the Hearing Aids icon, touch your AirPods or hearing aids, and then touch the **Listen Live** button.

(If you can't find the Hearing Devices button, you can add it to the Controls Centre, simply enter the Settings application, touch Controls Centre, and then select Hearing.)

→ Put your iPad close to the audio source.

CHAPTER 3

SIRI

Talking to Siri can be an easy way to get things done on your device. You can tell Siri to help you to translate a sentence, look for a place, set alarm, etc.

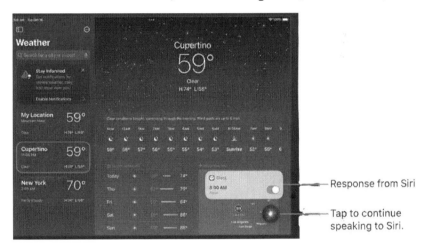

Response from Siri

Tap to continue speaking to Siri.

Configure Siri

If you didn't configure Siri when setting up your device, simply navigate to the Settings application, touch Siri and Search, and then carry out any of the below:

→ Enable the **Listen for "Hey Siri"** feature if you would like to summon Siri with your voice

→ Enable the Press **Top Button for Siri** feature if you would like to use a button to summon Siri

Summon Siri

→ You can summon Siri by long-press your iPad's top button or by saying **Hey Siri**

→ When Siri appears on your screen, simply request for something
You could say "What is 15% of 100" or "Play Flowers by Miley Cyrus"

→ To ask for something else, simply touch the Listen icon

Note: If Siri did not get the request you made clearly, simply touch the Listen icon & rephrase your request

Or, you can touch the Listen icon and spell out part of your request. For instance, you can say "Call", and then spell the name of the person.

Type instead of talking to Siri

➜ Navigate to the Settings application and touch Accessibility
➜ Touch Siri and then activate the **Type to Siri** feature.
➜ To request for something, summon Siri, then type what you want in the text field.

Change Siri settings on your device

Navigate to the Settings application, touch Siri and Search, and then carry out any of the below:

➜ Deactivate the **Listen for "Hey Siri"** feature to stop Siri from responding to the **Hey Siri** voice request.
➜ Deactivate the **Press Top Button for Siri** feature to stop Siri from responding to the top button
➜ Deactivate the **Allow Siri When Locked** feature to stop Siri from responding when your device is locked
➜ To change the language Siri responds to, touch the **Language** button, then choose any of the available languages.

→ Change Siri's Voice: Touch the **Siri Voice** option, then select one of the available voices
→ Always display Siri's response on your screen: Touch the **Siri Response** button, then activate the **Always Show Siri's Captions** feature
→ Display your request on your screen: Touch the **Siri Response** button, then activate the **Always Show Speech** feature

Restrain Siri with your voice

Navigate to the Settings application, touch Siri and Search, disable the **Listen for "Hey Siri"** feature, then activate the **Listen for "Hey Siri"** feature again

CHAPTER 4

APPLE PAY

You can use Apple Pay to pay for items in applications & on sites that are compatible with Apple Pay.

Add a card

To add a credit or debit card, simply adhere to the directives below:

➔ Navigate to the Settings application, and touch Wallet and Apple Pay
➔ Touch the **Add Card** option. You may be prompted to log in with your Apple ID.
➔ Carry out any of the below:
  - Add a new card: Click on the **Debit or Credit Card** option, touch the **Continue** button, then scan your card or fill in your card information manually.
  - Add an old card: Touch the **Previous card** button, and then select a card you've previously used. It could be a card that's associated with your Apple ID or a card you've removed. Click on the **Continue**

button, verify with Touch ID, and insert the card's CVV number.

Your card provider will determine whether the card qualifies for Apple Pay and may request more info to finish the verification process.

View a card information & change its configuration

→ Navigate to the Settings application, and touch Wallet and Apple Pay.
→ Touch one of the cards, then carry out any of the below:
  • Click Transactions to see your history. Disable the **Show History** feature to hide this info. Check out your card issuer's statement to see your Apple Pay activity.
  • Delete your card from Apple Pay
  • Edit your billing address
  • Check out your card's last 4 digit

Change your Apple Pay settings

→ Navigate to the Settings application, and touch Wallet and Apple Pay.

➜ Carry out any of the below:
- Choose a default card
- Add contact info & the shipping address for purchases

Remove your card from Apple Pay if you misplace your iPad or if it's stolen

Carry out any of the below to remove your card from Apple Pay:

➜ On a PC or Mac: Simply log into your Apple ID account. Click on the **Lost iPad** option under **Devices**. Click on the **Remove Items** option under Wallet and Apple Pay.

➜ On another iPad or iPhone: Navigate to the Settings application, touch [your name], touch the **Lost iPad** option, then touch the **Remove Items** button in the Wallet and Apple Pay section.

➜ Call your cards issuer

Use Apple Pay in Application Clips, applications, & Safari on your device

You can use Apple Pay to pay for items in applications, Apps clip, & on the internet via Safari.

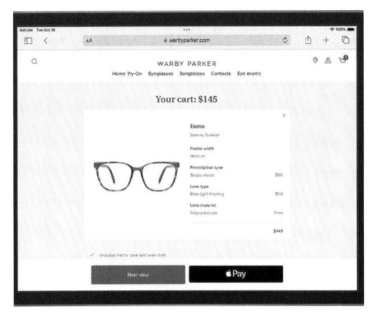

→ When checking out, touch the **Apple Pay** option.
→ Go through your payments details
  You can edit the shipping & billing addresses, and change your credit card, & contact details.
→ Confirm with Touch ID or insert your passcode

CHAPTER 5

FAMILY SHARING

The Family Sharing feature allows you & about 5 other individuals to share access to Apple services, iCloud storage plans, purchases, etc.

The organizer can invite other members to join the group. When members join the group, Family Sharing will be automatically setup on their devices. When someone accepts the offer to be part of the group they would immediately gain access to the shared content.

Set up a Family Sharing group

→ Navigate to the Settings application, touch [your name], click on Family Sharing and then adhere to the directives on your display to create a Family Sharing group.

→ Add members to the group. When adding an adult family member to the group, you can give the person the role of a guardian or parent.

→ Touch any of the features you would like to setup for your group, then adhere to the directives on your screen
To setup parental controls for a kid in the group, touch the child's name, touch the feature, and then adhere to the directives on your display.

Family Sharing features

You can setup or share the following features with your Family Sharing group:

→ Apps Store & Apple subscription
→ Purchases: You can share purchases from Apple TV, Apple Books, & Apps Store. All purchases are paid for by the organizer of the group.
→ Locations.
→ A device for your kid: You can setup an iPhone or iPad for a kid & personalize parental controls.
→ Parental control: You can manage what your kids buy online, how they make use of their devices, etc.
→ You can share your Apple Card with other group members

Add someone to the group

As the group organizer, you can add someone that has an Apple ID to the group.

→ Navigate to the Settings application, touch [your name], click on Family Sharing, and then click on the Add Members icon in the top right corner of your display.
→ Touch the **Invite Others** button, and then adhere to the directives on your display.
You can send invitations via Mail, Message, or AirDrop. If the person is close to you, simply touch the **Invite in Person** button and tell the

person to type their Apple ID details on your iPad

Creating an Apple ID for a kid

A parent, guardian, or the group organizer can setup an Apple ID for a child that is too young to create an Apple ID.

➜ Navigate to the Settings application, touch [your name], and then click on Family Sharing
➜ Carry out any of the below:
- If you are the group organizer: Click on the Add Members icon in the top right corner of your display, then touch the **Create Child Account** button
- If you are a guardian or parent: click on the Add Members icon in the top right corner of your display.
➜ Adhere to the directives on your display to complete the creation of the child's account.

Remove someone from the group

The group organizer can remove others from the group. When the group organizer removes someone from the group, the person will immediately lose access to the Family Sharing features.

➜ Navigate to the Settings application, touch [your name], and then click on Family Sharing

➜ Touch [the name of the member], and then click on Remove [name of the member] from Family.

You cannot remove a child from the group. But, you can transfer the child to a different group or delete their Apple ID.

Leave the family sharing group

After leaving a group, you will immediately lose access to the content you were sharing with the group.

➜ Navigate to the Settings application, touch [your name], and then click on Family Sharing

➜ Touch [your name], and then touch the **Stop Using Family Sharing** button

Disband a family sharing group

When the group organizer deactivates the group, all members are removed from the group at once. When the organizer disbands the group, all members will immediately lose access to the content they were sharing with the group.

➜ Navigate to the Settings application, touch [your name], and then click on Family Sharing

➜ Touch the **Stop Using Family Sharing** button

Share Apple subscription

➜ Navigate to the Settings application, touch [your name], and then click on Family Sharing

➜ Touch the **Subscriptions** button, then carry out any of the below:

- Touch any of the subscriptions you would like to share, and then adhere to the directives on your display.
- Touch the **Manage Subscriptions** button, then touch one of the subscriptions

Activate the Ask to Buy feature for a child

After setting up the Ask to Buy feature, a child in the group will have to ask for a parent, guardian, or the group organizer's approval before they can purchase anything online.

➔ Navigate to the Settings application, touch [your name], and then click on Family Sharing
➔ Touch the name of the child you plan on setting up the Ask to Buy feature for
➔ Touch the **Ask To Buy** button, then adhere to the directives on your display

CHAPTER 6

DOWNLOAD APPLICATIONS FROM THE APPS STORE

You can find applications, in-application events, & tips & tricks in the Apps Store.

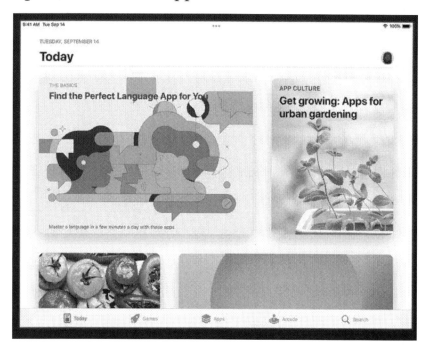

Note: Your iPad has to be connected to the internet & needs to have an Apple ID before you can make use of the Apps Store.

Find applications

Touch one of the tabs below:

➜ Today: Check out stories, & applications.
➜ Games.
➜ Apps.
➜ Arcade.
➜ Search: Type what you want, then touch the Search button on your keyboard.

Learn more about an application

Touch one of the apps to view the following info & more:

➜ In-application event
➜ Size of the file
➜ Support for other Apple devices
➜ Privacy info
➜ Family Sharing & Game Centre compatibility
➜ Screenshots
➜ Review & ratings
➜ Supported languages

Buy & download an application

➜ Click on the price. Touch the **Get** button If the application is free.

If there is a Redownload button☁ instead of a price, it means you've purchased the application already and it downloaded it for free.

➜ If necessary, verify with Touch ID, or your password.

Give or share an application

➜ Click on the application to view its info.
➜ Click on the Share button⬆, then select one of the sharing options or click on the **Gift Application** button

Redeem or send an Apple Gift Card

➜ Click on the Account button⊙ or your photo at the upper right part of your display
➜ Touch any of the below:
  • Send Gift Card via E-mail
  • Redeem Gift Code or Card

CHAPTER 7

CAMERA

In this chapter, you will learn how to snap nice pictures with the Camera application.

Take pictures

Photos mode is the default mode you see when you launch the Camera application. You can capture still pictures with Photos mode. Simply swipe the selector down or up to select another mode, like Slo-mo, Pano, Video, etc.

➜ To open the camera in photo mode, tap Camera on the home screen or swipe left on the lock screen.
➜ Touch the White Shutter to snap a picture. You can also press one of the volume buttons to snap a picture.

You can set a timer by touching the Timer button⟳ , and then touching 10s or 3s.

To zoom, simply pinch open on your camera screen to zoom in or pinch close to zoom out

For your safety, you'll see a green dot at the upper part of your display when your Camera is being used.

Capture a panoramic picture

➜ Swipe the mode selector to select Pano mode and then touch the White Shutter.

➔ Move slowly in the arrow's direction
Ensure the arrow remains in the middle line
while you pan

➔ Touch the White Shutter when you are done.

Touch the arrow to move in the other direction. Turn your device to landscape orientation to pan vertically.

Take Burst photos

Burst mode captures many high-speed shots, so you have several shots to select from.

→ Swipe the mode selector to Square mode or Photos mode.
→ Long-press the white shutter to capture rapid-fire pictures.
  The counter displays the number of photos you've taken.
→ Raise your finger to stop
→ Click on the Burst thumbnail, then touch the **Select** button to select the images you would like to save.
  Gray dots under the thumbnails indicate recommended images to save.
→ Touch the circle in the bottom right edge of each picture you would like to store as a separate picture, and then touch the **Done** button.

To erase the whole group of Burst pictures, click the thumbnail, and then click on the delete icon 🗑.

Capture a Live Picture

A Live Photo snaps what takes place before & after taking your picture, as well as the audio.

➜ Select Photos mode.

➜ Click on the Live Photo button ◎ to enable or disable Live Photo.

➜ Touch the Shutter to snap the picture.

In your albums, Live Photos have a "Live" tag in them at the upper part of your display.

Take a selfie

Take a picture with your front-facing camera

➜ Enter the Camera application, and then touch the Switch Camera icon ● to use the front-facing camera.

➜ Keep your device in front of you.

➜ Touch the Shutter button to take pictures with the front-facing camera
You can also press one of the volume buttons to snap a picture.

Record a video

→ Swipe the mode selector to Video mode.
→ Click on the Record button to start & stop recording.
To zoom, simply pinch open on your camera screen to zoom in or pinch close to zoom out

Record a slow-motion video

When recording videos in slo-mo mode, the video is recorded as normal and you can see the slow-motion effect when you play it.

→ Swipe the mode selector to Slo-mo mode.
→ Click on the Record button to start & stop recording.
To slow down part of the video and set the rest to constant speed, click on the video thumbnail and then click on the **Edit** button. Drag the vertical bar at the bottom of the frame viewer to specify the segment you would like to play in slow motion.

To change the slo-mo recording setting, enter the Settings application, touch Camera, then touch Slo-mo recording.

Take a timelapse video

➔ Swipe the mode selector to Timelapse mode.
➔ Setup your device wherever you want to capture sunsets, traffic, or other experiences over a period.
➔ Click on the Record button to start & stop recording.

Mirror the front-facing camera

To capture a mirrored sefie that takes the picture as you see it in the Camera, simply enter the Settings application, touch Camera, then activate Mirror Front Camera.

View your pictures

All the videos & pictures captured in the Camera application are stored in the Photos application.

➔ In the Camera application, touch the thumbnail picture under the Shutter.
➔ Swipe to view your recent photos.
➔ Click on the **All Photos** button to view all your videos & pictures stored in the Photos application.

Share & print your pictures

➜ While checking out a picture, click on the Share button.

➜ Choose one of the sharing options like Messages, Mail, or AirDrop to share your photos.

➜ To print a picture, swipe up and touch the **Print** button from the actions list

Use Live Text with your camera

The Camera application can identify text & info found in the camera frame, allowing you to interact with them in many ways. You can highlight text to translate, share, or copy, or quickly carry out tasks like making a call, opening a site, or converting money.

You can use the Live Text feature in applications like Quick Look, Photos, Safari, etc.

→ Launch the Camera application, then set your device in a way that the text can be seen clearly on the camera frame.

→ Click on the Live Text button.

→ Long-press the text, then highlight the text with the grab points and carry out any of the actions below:
  • Copy the Text and paste it into other apps
  • Select all the text
  • Look Up: View web recommendations
  • Translate the text
  • Search the web
  • Share text via one of the sharing options

→ Touch the Live Text icon to go back to the Camera application

To disable the Live Text feature on your device camera, enter the Settings application, touch

Camera, and then deactivate the **Show Detected Text** feature.

Use the Camera app to scan QR codes

➜ Launch the Camera application, then set your device in a way that the code can be seen clearly on your screen.
➜ Touch the onscreen notification to access the appropriate site or application.

Interact with pictures using Live Text

When viewing an image in the Photos application, the Live Text feature identifies the text & info in the photo and lets you interact with it in many ways. You can highlight texts to copy, translate, share, or use quick actions to carry out tasks like making a call, opening a site, or converting money.

Copy, lookup & translate texts in a video or picture

Before you can make use of the Live Text feature, ensure you have activated it for all supported languages.

→ Enter the Settings application, touch the **General** button, then touch Language and Regions
→ Activate the Live Text feature.

Copy, translate & lookup text in a video or picture

→ Open one of the photos or pause a video that has text in it.
→ Click on the Live Text button, and then Long-press the selected text.
→ Highlight specific text using the grab points, then carry out any of the below:
  - **Copy text** to paste in other applications
  - **Select All** to highlight all the text
  - Look Up: View web recommendations
  - Translate the text
  - Search the web
  - Share text via one of the sharing options
→ Touch the Live Text icon to go back to the video or picture

Use quick actions to perform tasks in a video or picture

Depending on the picture or the video's content, you can touch one of the quick actions in the lower part of your screen to perform things like making a call, getting directions, translating languages, converting from one currency to another, etc.

➔ In the Photos application, open any of the pictures or pause a video that has text in it.
➔ Touch the Live Text button ☷
➔ Touch one of the quick actions in the lower part of your display
➔ Touch the Live Text icon ● to go back to the video or picture

Use Visual Look-Up to identify items in your pictures

The Visual Lookup feature allows iPad users to identify & get more info about famous landmarks, pets, plants, and more items that can be found in your pictures in the Photos application.

➔ In the Photos application, open one of the pictures in full screen; A checked Info button ⓘ shows that there is Visual Look Up info for that picture.
➔ Touch the Visual Lookup button ⓘ

➜ Touch the icon that pops-up in the picture or at the upper part of the picture info results to see Siri's Knowledge & more info about the object.

➜ Touch the picture to close the Visual Lookup results, and then touch the Close icon to close the picture info.

Lift subjects from the picture background

In the Photos application, you can remove a picture's subject from its background and then copy or share it in other applications.

➜ Open one of the photos in the Photos application.
➜ Briefly long-press the photo's subject. When the subject is outlined, carry out any of the below:
- Click on the **Copy** button, then paste the subject into a note, message, or e-mail.
- Click on the **Share** button, and then select any of the sharing options, like Mail, AirDrop, etc.

CHAPTER 8

MAIL

You can write, reply, send & receive emails from any of your e-mail accounts.

Change mailboxes or accounts.

Delete, move, or mark multiple messages.

Move message to another mailbox.

Add an email account

When you launch the Mail application for the first time, you would be prompted to setup an e-mail account—simply adhere to the directives on your display.

To add another e-mail account, adhere to the directives below:

➔ Navigate to the Settings application, touch Mail, touch Accounts, and then touch Add Accounts.
➔ Carry out any of the below:
  • Click on any of the e-mail services - for instance, Microsoft Exchange or iCloud - and then type your e-mail account info.
  • Touch the **Other** button, touch the **Add Mail Account** button, then type your e-mail account details.

Sign out or remove e-mail accounts

➔ Navigate to the Settings application, touch Mail, and then touch Accounts.
➔ Click on the e-mail account you plan on removing, then carry out any of the below:
  • If you want to remove an iCloud e-mail account: Click on the **iCloud** button, click on iCloud Mail, and then disable the Use on this iPad feature.
  • If you want to remove any other e-mail account: Disable Mail.

Note: If you want to remove the e-mail account from all applications on your device, click on the **Delete Account** button.

Read an e-mail

Touch any of the e-mails in your mail-box list.

Use the Remind Me feature to get back to an email later

If you do not have time to deal with an e-mail immediately, you can choose a date & time to get a reminder and bring the message to the top of your inbox.

Touch the Reply button⤺ at the lower right part of the e-mail, click on the **Remind Me** button, and select a reminder time.

Preview an e-mail & a list of options

In your mail box list, long-press an e-mail to preview the email's content & view a list of options for replying, moving it, etc.

Show a longer preview of your emails

A normal preview only shows 2 lines of text for emails. You can decide to view more lines without having to open the e-mail.

Navigate to the Settings application, touch Mail, touch Preview in the Messages List section, and then select up to 5 lines.

Write an email

➔ Click on the Compose button ☑ .

➔ Tap in the e-mail, and then write what you want.

➔ Touch the Format button Aa at the top of your keyboard to change the format.
  You can use a different text colour & font style, use an italic or bold style, add a numbered or bulleted list, etc.

➔ Touch the Send icon ⬆ to send your e-mail.

Tap to send the message, or touch and hold to schedule a time to send it later.

Add a recipient

➔ Click on the **To** field, then write the recipients' names.
While typing, the Mail application will automatically suggest people in your Contacts list, along with e-mail addresses for those who have multiple e-mail addresses.

Touch the Add Contacts icon⊕ to enter the Contacts application & add recipients from your contacts.

→ If you would like to send a copy to others, click on the Cc/ Bcc field and then carry out any of the below:

- Click on the Cc box, and type the names of the individuals you would like to send a copy to.
- Touch the Bcc box, then type the names of the individuals whose names you do not want the other recipients to see

Snap an e-mail address from an image

The Live Text feature allows iPad users to interact with e-mail addresses found on a poster, business card, etc. using the Photos application. With this feature, you can easily start e-mails without having to enter the e-mail address manually.

→ Open an image/picture in the Photos application, then touch the e-mail address you plan on capturing.

→ When you see a yellow frame around the visible text, click on the Live Text button.

→ Select the e-mail address using the grab points, then touch the **New Mail Message** button.

Schedule an e-mail to send later

Long-press the Send button⬆, then select when you want the email to be sent.

Click on the **Send Later** button to view other options.

Send e-mail from another account

If you have multiple e-mail accounts, you can choose which account to send an e-mail from.

➜ When drafting the email, touch the Cc/ Bcc, From field.
➜ Touch the From field, then select one of your accounts

Unsend emails

You've got about 10 seconds to change your mind after sending an e-mail.

Touch the **Undo Send** button at the lower part of your display to unsend the e-mail.

You can give yourself more than 10 seconds to change your mind, simply enter the Settings application, touch Mail, touch the **Undo Send Delay** option, then select how long you want outgoing emails to be delayed.

Reply to an e-mail

→ Touch in the e-mail, then carry out any of the below:
  - Touch the More Actions icon to reply to only the sender
  - Touch the Reply All button to reply to the sender & other recipients
→ Write what you want, then touch the Send button to send the message

Forward emails

You can forward an email to other recipients.

→ Touch in the e-mail, and then touch the Forward button
→ Type the new recipient's e-mail addresses

➔ Touch in the e-mail, then write what you want. You will see the forwarded message under.

Follow up on e-mails

If you send an email & do not get a response from the recipients for a few days, the e-mail automatically goes to the top of your inbox so you don't forget to follow up.

Navigate to the Settings application, touch Mail, then activate or deactivate Follow-Up Suggestions.

Attach pictures, videos, or documents to email

You can add & send videos, images, & documents in your e-mails for easy download & storage for your recipients.

➔ Touch where you want to add the file in the email, then carry out any of the below:
  • Insert a document: Click on the Insert Attachment button⬜ on your keyboard, then find the document in the Files application.

In the Files application, touch the Recent or Browse button, then touch a folder, location, or file to open it.

- Add a saved video or picture: Click on the Add Photo or Video Actions button  at the top of the keyboard, then click on the **Photo Library** button. Select one of your photos or videos.

- Capture a video or picture & insert it in the e-mail: Touch the Photo or Video Actions button 📷 at the top of the keyboard, click on the **Take Photo or Video** button, then capture a picture or record a video. Touch the **Use Video** or the **Use Photo** button to add the file to your e-mail, or touch the **Retake** button if you want to take another shot.

Scan the document and attach it to the email

You can scan a document & send it in PDF format.

➜ Touch where you want to add the scanned file in the email, then touch the Photo or Video Actions button 📷 at the top of the keyboard

➜ Touch the **Scan Document** button, then set your device in a way that the document page can be seen clearly on your screen—your device will automatically capture the page

Simply touch the Capture button ⭕ to manually capture the page.

➜ Scan more pages, then touch the **Save** button when you are finished

➔ To make other adjustments to the saved file, touch the document, then carry out any of the below:

- Touch the Filter button  to use a filter
- Touch the Crop button ⊹ to crop the document
- Touch the Rotate button ↻ to rotate the file
- Touch the Trash button 🗑 to delete the document

Download attachments sent to you

Long-press the attachment, then select the **Save to Files** or the **Save Image** option.

If you pick the **Save Image** option, you can find the file in the Photos application. If you pick the **Save to Files** option, you can find the file in the Files application.

Tip: To open an attachment with any other application, click on the Share button⬆ & select the application.

Annotate e-mail attachments on your device

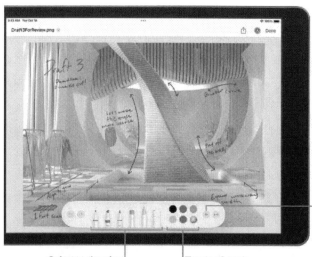

Tap to add text, shapes, and signatures, or use the Magnifier.

Select a drawing tool, the eraser, or the selection tool.

Tap to choose colors.

In the mail application, you can write & draw on a picture, PDF attachment, or video, and then save it on your device or send it back.

➜ In the e-mail, touch the attachment, then touch the Markup icon Ⓐ

➜ Select any of the tools available in the drawing tools, then use your finger to draw

➜ When you are done, touch the **Done** button, then you can store, discard, or send the edited file

Change your mail notifications

➜ Navigate to the Settings application, touch Mail, touch Notifications, and then ensure you've activated the **Allow Notifications** feature.

➜ Touch the **Customize Notification** button, then click on the e-mail account you plan to make adjustments to.

➜ Choose the settings you want, such as Badges or Alerts. When you activate the Alerts feature, you can personalize your sound by choosing a different ringing tone or alert tone.

Search for e-mail in the Mail application

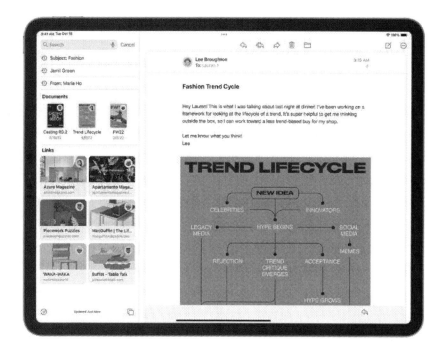

→ Swipe down from the center of a mail box to open the search box.

→ Touch the search box & write a text that can be found in the email.

→ Select the **Current Mailbox** or the **All Mailboxes** option at the upper part of the results list.

→ Click on the **Search** button and then click on one of the emails in the results list to read it.

Check e-mails from one account at a time

If you have more than one e-mail account with the mail application, you can use the mail-boxes list to check out e-mails from any of your accounts.

Touch the Show Sidebar button in the top left part of your display, then touch any of the mailboxes in the E-mail Account section you would like to access.

The mailboxes listed under a specific e-mail account only show e-mails from that e-mail account. For instance, to see only e-mails sent from your iCloud account, click on iCloud and then click on the **Sent** button.

Filter emails

In the Mail application, you can use the mail filters to temporarily display specific messages that meet the criteria you choose in the filter list. For instance, if you choose Unread mail & Only Mail with attachments, the mail list will just display unread e-mails with attachments.

➔ Touch the Filter button in the lower left part of the mail-box list.
Note: When going through an e-mail on your device in Portrait orientation, click on the Show

Sidebar button⊞ to show the e-mail list with the Filter button⊜ at the lower part of your display.

➜ Click on the **Filtered By** button, then choose or activate the criteria for the e-mails you want to see.
➜ To hide e-mails that do not match the current filter, click on the Filter button⊜ in the lower left corner. Touch once more to disable the filter.

Touch the Filter button⊜ to disable all filters. To disable a certain filter, click on the "Filter by" button and then unselect it.

Protect email privacy on iPad

The Mail Privacy Protection feature makes it difficult for senders to get info about your Mail activities. It conceals your IP address so that email senders cannot track your other online activities or pinpoint your location. It also stops the sender from knowing if you have opened the e-mail they sent to you.

➜ Navigate to the Settings application, touch Mail, and then touch Privacy Protections.
➜ Activate the Protect Mail Activity feature.

Personalize your e-mail signature

You can set up an e-mail signature that will automatically appear at the lower part of every e-mail you're sending.

➔ Navigate to the Settings application, touch Mail, and then click Signature in the Composing section.
➔ Touch the text box, and then edit your signature. You can only make use of text in your e-mail signature.

Tip: If you have multiple e-mail accounts, click on the **Per Account** button to create a unique signature for each of your accounts.

Delete emails

Carry out any of the below to delete e-mails:

➔ While going through an e-mail, touch the Trash button at the upper part of the e-mail.
➔ While going through your e-mail list, swipe left on an e-mail, then touch the **Trash** button
➔ Delete more than one email at the same time: While going through an emails list, touch the

Edit button, choose the e-mails you would like to delete, then touch the **Trash** button

Recover deleted emails

→ Touch the sidebar button to see your mailboxes, then touch the account's Trash mail-box.
→ Click on the e-mail you would like to restore.
→ Click on the Copy button , and then choose the mail-box you would like to move the e-mail to.

Tip: If you want to see deleted e-mails from all your accounts, click on **Mail-boxes**, click on the **Edit** button, and then choose the All Trash Mail box.

Print emails

Click on the More Actions icon , then click on the **Print** button.

Print a photo or attachment

Touch the attachment to see it, touch the Share button , then select the **Print** button

CHAPTER 9

BROWSE WITH SAFARI

With the Safari application, you can surf the internet, visit sites, preview site links, translate web pages, etc.

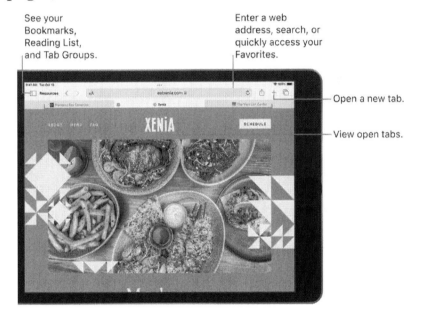

See your Bookmarks, Reading List, and Tab Groups.

Enter a web address, search, or quickly access your Favorites.

Open a new tab.

View open tabs.

View sites

In the Safari application, you can easily surf through a page with some taps.

➔ Return to top: Touch the top edge of your display twice to quickly go back to the beginning of a long webpage.

➔ Rotate your device to landscape orientation to see more of the webpage.
➔ Drag down from the upper part of the webpage to refresh the webpage
➔ Touch the Share icon  at the upper right corner of the webpage to share a link

View pages in Split View

The Split View feature allows you to open 2 webpages side by side in the Safari application.

→ Open a webpage in Splits view: Long-press the Tabs icon ⧉, and then touch the **New Window** button.
→ Open a web link in Splits view: Long-press the link, then touch the **Open in New Windows** button.
→ Move a window to the other half of your screen: Long-press the Safari Multitasking Controls button ••• at the upper part of the window, then drag to the right or left part of your screen.

→ Long-press the Tabs icon ⧉ to close tabs in a Splits view window
→ You can leave Splits View by simply dragging the middle divider over the window you plan on closing

Preview site links

Long press a link in the Safari application to view the link's preview without having to open the webpage. To open the link, touch the **Open** button or simply touch the preview.

Touch outside the preview to close the preview & remain on the current webpage.

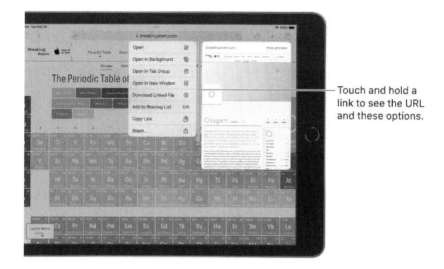

Touch and hold a link to see the URL and these options.

Translate a page

When viewing a website that is in a different language, you can use the Safari application to translate the page.

Click on the Page Settings button AA, and then click on the Translation button.

Manage downloads

Click on the Download button to see the status of your download, to quickly gain access to a downloaded file, and more.

Change the text size

➔ Touch the Site Settings button A𝖠 in the search box.

➔ Touch the big **A** to make the font size larger or the small **A** to reduce the font size

Change screen & privacy controls

With Page Settings, you can switch to Readers view, conceal the search bar, set privacy controls for a site, etc.

Click the Page Settings button AA, then carry out any of the below:

→ Touch the **Show Reader** option to get a streamlined view of the page.
Touch the **Hide Reader** button to go back to the regular view

→ Touch the **Hide Toolbar** option to conceal the search box (touch the top of your display to reveal it).

→ Touch the **Request Desktop Website** option to see how the site looks on a computer.

→ Touch the **Website Settings** option to customize privacy & display controls for every time you go to the site

Change the Safari layout

You can pick the Safari layout that works for you.

➜ Launch the Settings application, touch Safari, and then scroll to Tabs.

➜ Choose Compact Tab Bar or Separate Tab Bar.

Browse websites

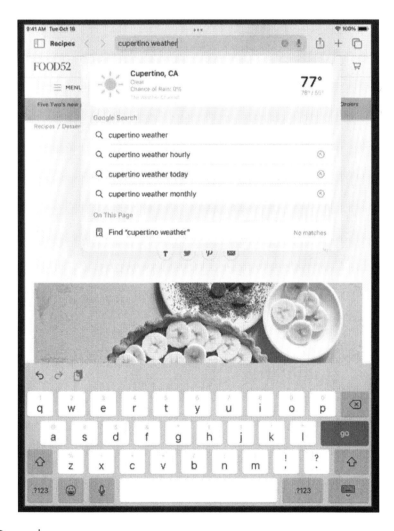

→ Type a word, URL, or phrase in the search box.
→ Touch one of the search suggestions, or touch the **Go** button on your keyboard

If you do not want Safari to show search suggestions, enter the Settings application, touch Safari, then disable the Search Engine Suggestions feature in the Search section.

Search the page

You can look for a phrase or word on a web page.

→ Click on the Share button⬆️, and then touch the **Find on Page** button.
→ Type the phrase or word in the search box
→ Touch the More button∨ to see more instances.

Open a link in a new tab

Tabs allow you to surf through many open pages

To open a link in a new tab, long-press the link, then touch the **Open in Background** button.

See a tab history

You can view the pages you've visited in the past in this tab. Long-press the Back icon ‹ or the Forward icon ›.

Close a tab

Touch the Tab icon ⬚, then touch the Close button ⊗ in the upper right corner of the tab.

Open a tab you closed recently

Long-press the New Tab button✛, and then select
it from the list of closed tabs.

Create a Tab Group

In Safari, create Tab Groups to keep tabs arranged
& easy to find later.

→ To create a new Tab group, click the Show
Sidebar button⬚ to reveal the side bar, then
click on the Groups Tab button⊞ in the upper
part of the side bar.

➔ Select any of the options, and then give the Tab Group a name.

Move a tab to another Tab Group

➔ Long-press in the tab bar, then touch the **Move to Tab Group** option.
➔ Select a Tab Group you've created, or touch the **New Tab Group** button to create a tab group.

Annotate & store a webpage in PDF format

You can markup, draw & write notes on a webpage and share it with others in PDF format.

→ Click the Share button ⬆.

→ Click on the **Markup** button Ⓐ, then select a tool to mark up the web page.

→ Click on the **Done** button, and then adhere to the directives on your display to store the page in PDF format

Block pop-ups

Launch the Settings application, touch Safari, then activate the **Block Pop-ups** feature

Clear the cache on your device

To clear the cache on your device, simply clear your browsing data & history. This will remove the history of sites you've visited. This step clears cookies & deletes the permissions you've given sites to use your location or send you messages.

→ In the Safari application, click the Show Sidebar button ⬜.

➔ Touch the History option, and then touch the **Clear** button

➔ Select the history you want to delete

Visit websites privately

When you open tabs in the Private Browsing mode, the sites you visit will not appear in your Browsing History.

To enter the Private mode, click on the Show Sidebar button⬛, and then touch the **Private** button

When you enter Private Browsing mode, the Safari app background will become gray & the website you enter won't appear in your browsing History.

To hide the website & leave the Private Browsing mode, click on the Show Sidebar button⬛ and switch to another Tab group. You will see the tabs when next you use the Private Browsing mode.

CHAPTER 10

FACETIME

You can make Audio & Video calls with the FaceTime application.

Configure FaceTime

➔ Navigate to the Settings application, touch Face-Time, type your Apple ID details, and then touch the **Sign-in** button
➔ Activate FaceTime if you haven't already, then carry out any of the below:
  • Share your screen in calls: Touch the **SharePlay** button, then activate the Shareplay feature.
  • Activate Speaking to highlight the person talking in calls
  • Show captions in calls: Activate the Live Captions feature.
  • Activate FaceTime Live Photos to capture Live Pictures in calls

Create a Face-Time call link

Create a link to a Face-Time call & share the link with friends via Messages or Mail, which they can use to participate in the Face-Time call.

➔ Enter the FaceTime application, and click on the **Create link** button at the upper part of your display.
➔ Select one of the sharing options to send the link.

Note: You can send the link to anybody even those that do not have Apple devices. They can join the call from their browser, no login is required.

Make FaceTime calls

Your device has to be connected to the internet before you can make & receive FaceTime calls.

Turn off your video

Turn off your mic.

➜ Enter the FaceTime application, touch the **New FaceTime** button at the upper part of your display

➜ Write the phone number or name of the individual you would like to call in the entry box at the upper part of your display, then touch the **Video** button to make a video call or the **Voice** button to make a voice call.

Or, touch the Add Contact icon ⊕ to launch the Contacts application and start your call; or touch one of the suggested contacts in your call history.

Receive FaceTime calls

When someone calls you via FaceTime, carry out one of the below:

Send the caller a text message.

Set up a reminder to return a call.

➜ Touch the **Accept** button to accept the call.

➜ Touch the **Decline** button to reject the call

➜ Touch the **Remind Me** button to set a reminder to call the person back.

➜ Touch the **Message** button to send the caller a text message

Delete calls from your calls history

In the Face-Time application, simply swipe left on a call in your calls history and then touch the **Delete** button.

Take Live Photos in FaceTime calls

While making a FaceTime video call, you can capture a Live Picture to snap a moment of the discussion. The camera snaps everything that happens before & after taking the shot, plus the sound, so you can see and hear it as it happened afterward.

Before you can capture Live Photos with the FaceTime application, first ensure you've activated FaceTime Live Photos in the Settings application> FaceTime, and then carry out any of the below:

➔ Touch the Capture button ⭕ to take a Live Photo while on a single-person call

➔ While on a Group call: Touch the person's tile, touch the Full Screen button ⬉, then touch the Capture button ⭕

You and the person will receive an alert that the picture was taken, and you can find the picture in the Photos application

Activate Live Captions

While making a Face-Time video call, you can activate the **Live Captions** feature so that the conversation can be converted to text & shown in real-time on your screen. If you have trouble hearing what the other person is saying in the call, the Live Captions feature can make it easy for you to follow along.

➔ While on a video call, touch your screen to display the call controls (if you cannot see them).

➔ Click on the Info button ⓘ at the upper part of the controls, activate **Live Captions**, then touch the **Done** button.

The Live Captions window will appear at the upper part of your screen, displaying the call's auto-transcribed dialog & the person talking.

To disable the Live Captions feature, simply click on the Info button ⓘ at the upper part of your display, then deactivate **Live Captions**.

Use other applications while on a FaceTime call

While making a FaceTime call, you can make use of other applications—for instance, to calculate something, etc.

Swipe up from the lower edge of your display to enter your iPad's Home Screen and then touch an application icon to launch the application.

To go back to the Face-Time screen, touch the green bar at the upper part of your display.

Start a group FaceTime call

You can have up to 32 individuals participating in a Face-Time group call.

➜ Enter the FaceTime application, touch the **New FaceTime** button at the upper part of your display

➜ Write the phone numbers or names of the individuals you would like to call in the entry box at the upper part of your display, then touch the **Video** button to make a video call or the **Voice** button to make a voice call.

Or, touch the Add Contacts icon⊕ to launch the Contacts application and add people; or touch one of the suggested contacts in your call history.

Tap to add more people to the call.

Each person participating in the call will appear in a tile on your screen. When someone starts talking or you touch a tile, that tile will become more prominent. Swipe through the row to find a participant you can't see.

To stop the speaker's tile from getting bigger in a Group Face-Time call, enter the Settings application, touch FaceTime, and then disable Speaking in the **Automatic Prominence** segment.

Add someone to the call

Anyone participating in the FaceTime call can add other people at any time to the call.

➜ While on Face-Time call, touch your screen to display the call controls (if you cannot see them), click on the Info button ⓘ at the upper part of the controls, then touch the **Add People** button.

➜ Write the phone number, name, or Apple ID of the individual you would like to call in the entry box at the upper part of your display.

Or, touch the Add Contact icon ⊕ to add somebody from your Contacts list.

➜ Touch the **Add People** button

Leave a Group FaceTime call

Touch the **Leave** button to exit the call

View FaceTime participants in a grid format

In a Group FaceTime call, you can view those participating in the call in equal-sized tiles on a grid layout. The Speaker's tile is automatically distinguished so that you can easily know who's speaking

While on a Face-Time call, touch the **Grid** button at the upper right part of your display.

Touch the **Grid** button one more time to turn off the feature.

Share your screen in a FaceTime call

The SharePlay feature allows you to share the content on your screen in a FaceTime call—bringing applications, sites, etc. into the conversation.

➔ While on a Face-Time Group call, touch your screen to display the call controls (if you cannot see them), touch the Share Content icon , and then touch the **Share My Screen** button.
Your screen will appear in the FaceTime call for everybody to see after three seconds
➔ Swipe up from the lower edge of your display to enter your iPad's Home Screen and then launch

an application, open a website, or a document you would like to share in the call.

Click on the Share content icon🖼 once more to stop screen sharing.

Transfer FaceTime calls to other devices

While on a Face-Time call, you can transfer the call from your device to another device that you are logged in with your Apple ID.

Note: Your contact info selected for the call, listed in the Settings application> FaceTime (in the **You Can Be Reached By Face-Time At** section) needs to match the contact info selected in the Settings application> FaceTime on the device you want to transfer the call to.

➔ Ensure you've turned on the other device and then touch the screen that is showing the call.
  You will see a call notification on the Lock Screen or in the Notifications Center of the other device, as well as the suggestion **"Move call to this device"**.
➔ Touch the notification to transfer the call, or touch the Video Handoff button🔲 at the

upper part of your display, then touch the Switch icon `Switch` .
You'll see a preview of the call, displaying audio, microphone, & camera settings.

→ Ensure you setup the audio, Mic, & camera settings, then touch the Switch icon `Switch`
The call will move to your other device. A banner will appear on the original device letting you know that the call has been transferred, as well as the Switch icon `Switch`, which you can touch to move the call back.

Enable Center Stage

The Center Stage feature adjusts your iPad's front-facing camera to frame you while you move around the view field during a Face-Time video call.

→ While on a Face-Time video call, swipe down from the upper right corner of your screen to reveal the Controls Center.
→ Click on the **Video Effects** button, and then click on Centre Stage to activate the feature.
→ Touch Centre Stage once more to deactivate this feature

Blur the background

The Portrait mode feature blurs the background & places the visual focus on you.

➔ While making a Face-Time video call, touch your tile

➔ Touch the Portrait icon 🔘 in your tile

Touch the icon 🔘 once more to deactivate the feature.

Switch to the back camera

While making a Face-Time video call, touch your tile, and then touch the Camera icon 📷

Touch the icon 📷 once more to switch to the other camera.

Turn off the camera

Touch your screen, and then touch the Video icon 📹.

Touch the icon once more to turn on the camera

Filter out background noise

If you want the people on the call to hear your voice clearly, simply activate the Voice Isolation mode. This feature makes your voice the priority of the call & blocks out background noise.

➜ While on a Face-Time video call, swipe down from the upper right corner of your screen to reveal the Controls Center.
➜ Click on the **Mic Mode** button, and then click on Voice Isolation to activate the feature

Simply activate the Wide Spectrum mode if you want your voice & the noise around you to be heard in the call

Turn off the sound

Touch your screen, and then touch the Audio icon .

Touch the icon once more to turn on the sound.

Leave a Face-Time call

Touch your screen to display the call controls (if you cannot see them), then touch the Exit icon ⊗

Block unwanted FaceTime callers

You can block Face-Time calls from unwanted callers in the Face-Time application.

➜ In your Face-Time call history, click on the Info button ⓘ beside the e-mail address, number, or name of the contact you plan on blocking.

➜ Scroll, touch the **Block this Caller** button, and then touch the **Block Contacts** button.

To unblock one of your blocked contacts, click on the Info button ⓘ beside the e-mail address, number, or name of the contact in your call log, scroll, then touch the **Unblock this Caller** button.

CHAPTER 11

MAPS

You can see your location in the Maps app.

Allow Maps to use Location Services

To allow the Maps application to find your location & provide accurate directions, your device needs to have an internet connection, & Location Services has to be activated.

If the Maps app shows an alert that Location Services is disabled, touch the notification, touch the **Turn On in Setting** button, then activate Locations Service.

Show your current location

Click the Locate button �.

Where you are at the moment can be found in the center of the map. The upper part of the map is north. Touch the Control button ◢ to display where you're heading at the top instead of the north. Touch the Directional Control button ▲ or the Compass button ◉ to continue displaying the north at the top.

Select the correct map

The icon at the upper right part of the map shows whether the map you are on is for Transit🚊, driving🚗, satellite viewing🌐, or exploring🏔. To pick another map, adhere to the directives below:

➔ Click on the icon at the upper right part of the map.
➔ Select any other type of map, and then click on the Close icon✕.

View a 3D map

Carry out any of the below on a 2D map:

➔ Swipe up with 2 fingers.
➔ Touch the **3D** button at the upper right part of the Satellite map.
➔ In selected cities, click on the **3D** button at the upper right of the map.

On 3D Maps, you can:

➔ Drag 2 of your fingers down or up to change the angle.
➔ Zoom in to view buildings & other features.
➔ Touch the **2D** button close to the upper right part of the 3D map to go back to the 2D map

Rotate, zoom, or move a map or 3D globe

→ Drag a map to move around it.
→ Zoom in or out: pinch open on your screen to zoom in, and pinch close to zoom out.

   When zooming in on a 2D map, you'll see a scale at the upper part of the map. To change the Distance unit, navigate to the Settings application, touch Maps, then choose Kilometers or Miles.
→ Rotate the map: Use 2 of your fingers to long-press the map, then rotate your fingers.

   After rotating a map, click the Compass button 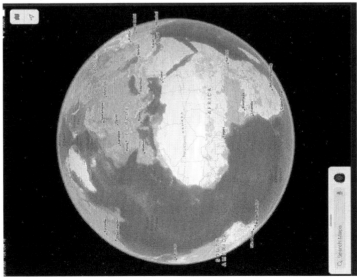 to display the North at the top of the map.
→ Explore the world with an interactive 3D globe: Keep zooming out of the map till it turns into a 3D globe. You can rotate the 3D globe by dragging it. Zoom out or in to see details of oceans, deserts, mountains, etc.

Find a place

Touch the Search box, and then type.

Here are different ways you can search for places in the Maps application:

➜ Area (Brooks)
➜ Intersection (9th & Markets)
➜ Landmark (Niagara Falls)
➜ Zip code (60623)
➜ Business (Apple Inc, movies, restaurants.)

When you see your search results, scroll down the list to view all of them. Touch one of the results to get more info about the location, or receive directions to the place.

CHAPTER 12

NOTES

In the Notes application, you can write down ideas or arrange detailed info with check-lists, pictures, web-links, scanned docs, etc.

Create & edit a note

➜ Click on the New Note button ⬕ and then start typing.
The note's 1st line will automatically become the name of the note.

➜ Click on the Format button Aa to change the format.
You can use a different font style, you can add a numbered or bulleted list, etc.

➜ Touch the **Done** button to save the note.

To add a checklist in a note, simply tap on the check-list button ⊙≡ and then start writing. Touch the Return key to go to the next item. Swipe to the left or right on an item to decrease or increase the item's indentation

To add a table in the note, tap on the Table button ⊞. To write in the table, just touch one of the cells, and start typing. Long press the shift button and touch next to go to another line. To remove a table & change the contents of the table to normal text, tap in a cell in the table, touch the Table Info button ⊞ and then touch the **Convert to Text** button

Write or draw in a note

You can draw or write in a note in the Notes application using your Apple Pencil or finger. You can pick from different Markup tools & colours.

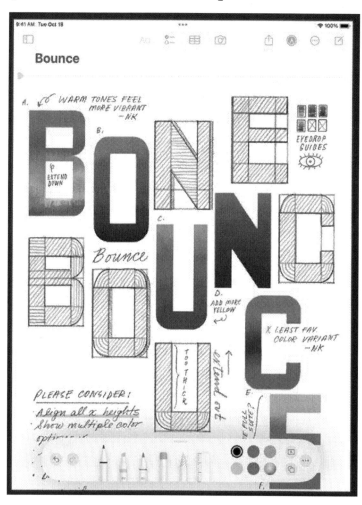

Write or draw in a note

➔ Use your Apple Pencil to write or draw in the note. Or touch the Markup button Ⓐ to use your finger to write or draw.
➔ Carry out any of the below:
- Use a different tool or colour: Select it from the Markup tools
- Drag the resize handle down or up to change the handwriting area.
- Change what you're writing with your Apple Pencil to typed text: Touch the Handwriting tool , then write with your Apple Pencil

Scan text into a note

You can use your camera to scan text & insert it in a note.

➔ In a note, click on the Camera button 🖻 and then click the **Scan Text** button.
➔ Set your device in a way that the text can be seen clearly within the Camera frame
➔ When you see the yellow frame around the visible text, touch the Live Text button 🔲
➔ Select the text using the grab points, then touch the **Insert** button

Scan documents

➜ In a note, click on the Camera button 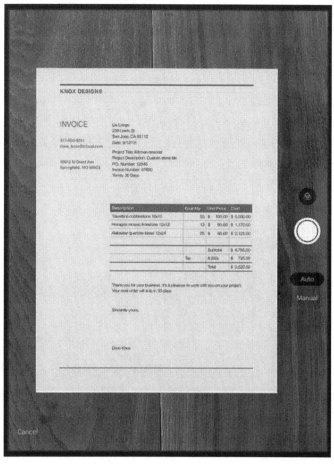 and then click the **Scan Documents** button.

➜ Set your device in a way that the document can be seen clearly on your screen; your device will automatically capture the document.

Touch the Capture button⭕ to manually capture the document.

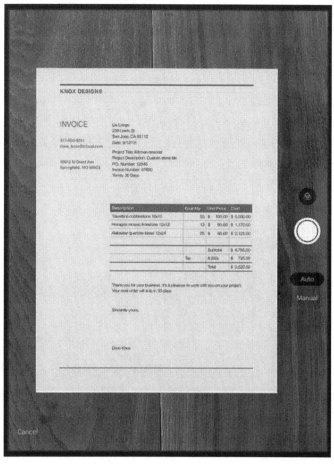

➔ Scan more pages, then touch the **Save** button when you are finished

➔ To make other adjustments to the saved file, touch the document, then carry out any of the below:

- Touch the Add button ⊕ to add more pages
- Touch the Filter button ⊛ to use a filter
- Touch the Crop button ⊐ to crop the document
- Touch the Rotate button ⊡ to rotate the file
- Touch the Trash button 🗑 to delete the document
- Markup the file: Touch the Share button ⬆, touch the Markup button Ⓐ, then make use of the Mark up tool to draw or write on the document

Add a video or picture

➔ Click on the Camera button 📷 in a note

➔ Select one of the videos or pictures from the Photos library, snap a new picture, or record a video.

➔ To change the attachment's preview size, long-press the attachment, then touch the **Large Image** or the **Small Image** button

Tip: To draw on an image, touch the picture, and then touch the Markup button Ⓐ.

To store videos & pictures captured in the Notes application in the Photos application, enter the Settings application, touch Notes, and then activate the **Save to Photos** feature.

See all attachments in the Notes app

➔ At the top of the list of notes, click the Folder Actions button ⊙ and then click on the **View Attachments** button to view thumbnails of docs, pictures, links, drawings, and more.
➔ To enter a note that has a specific attachment, touch the attachment thumbnail, then touch the **Show in Note** button.

Create Quick Notes

The Quick Notes feature allows you to write info over any application or screen on your device.

You can find your Quick Notes in the Notes application.

To begin a Quick Note from any application, carry out any of the below:

➜ Open the Controls Centre, then touch the Quick Notes button🔳

(If you can't find the Quick Notes button🔳, you can add it to the Controls Centre —enter the Settings application, touch Controls Centre, then select Quick Notes)

➜ Use the Apple Pencil or one of your fingers to swipe up from the lower right edge of your screen

View & organize your Quick Notes

To see all Quick Notes in the Notes application, click on Quick Notes in the folder list.

If a Quick Note is moved to a different folder, it will become a regular note & will not appear as one of the Quick Notes in the Notes application.

Search your notes

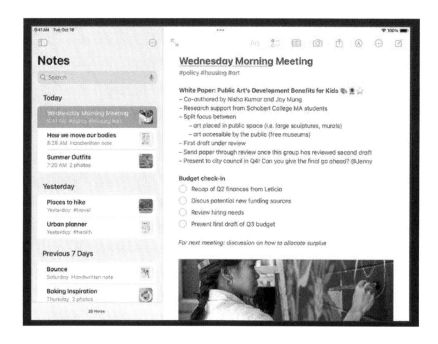

→ Drag down on the notes list to bring out the search box.

→ Touch the Search box, then type what you want.

Create, move, delete, or rename, a folder

Carry out any of the below in the folders list:

→ Create a folder: Click the New folder button 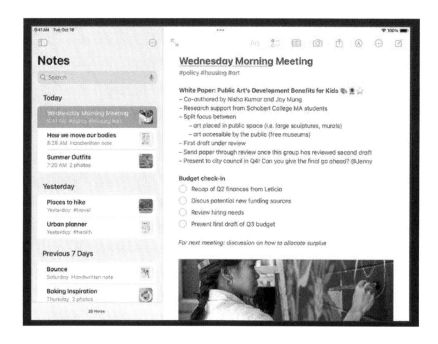, select one of your accounts (if you have multiple accounts), click on the **New Folder** button, and then give the folder a name.

→ You can create a subfolder by long-pressing a folder and then dragging it onto another folder.
→ Change the name of a folder: Long-press the folder, touch the **Rename** button, then change the name of the folder
→ You can move a folder by long-pressing the folder, and then dragging the folder to another location.
→ Delete a folder: Long-press the folder, and then touch the **Delete** button.

Delete a note

Long-press the note, then touch the **Delete** button

If you still want the note, simply open the Recently Deleted folder to get the note back.

Lock notes

You can lock your notes to safeguard important info.

Lock notes with your phone passcode

You can make use of your iPad's passcode to open your locked notes so that you would not need to create another password for the notes.

→ Navigate to the Settings application, touch Notes, and then touch Password.
→ If you have more than one account, select one of the accounts
→ Touch the **Use Device Passcode** button
→ You can activate Touch ID to use it to unlock your locked notes.

Lock notes with a special password

You can create a different password for your locked notes.

→ Navigate to the Settings application, touch Notes, and then touch Password.
→ If you have more than one account, select one of the accounts
→ Touch the **Use Custom Passcode** button
→ You can activate Touch ID to use it to unlock your locked notes.

If you forget your passcode, you can reset it but you will not be able to gain access to your previously locked notes. Enter the Settings application, touch

Notes, touch Password, and then touch Reset Password

Change the lock pattern

If you are making use of a standard password, you can switch to your device password. Enter the Settings application, touch Notes, touch Password, select one of your accounts if you have multiple accounts, and then touch the **Use Device Passcode** button.

After changing the locking pattern, the notes making use of the previous method are transferred to the new method.

Lock notes

➔ Open a note, and then touch the Note Actions button at the upper right part of your screen.
➔ Click on the **Lock** button.

After locking a note, the name will remain visible in the notes list.

To remove a lock, simply open the note, click on the Note Actions button and then click on the **Remove** button.

Open your locked notes

After unlocking a locked note, all the locked notes in that account will be unlocked for some minutes.

➜ Touch the note, then touch the **View Notes** button
➜ You can use your passcode or Touch ID to unlock the note.

Carry out any of the below to lock the notes again:

➜ Touch the lock button
➜ Touch the **Lock Now** button at the lower part of the notes list
➜ Lock your device
➜ Leave the Notes application

CHAPTER 13

PASSCODE & TOUCH ID

Set a Passcode

Setup a passcode that must be inserted to unlock your device when it's turned on or when you wake it.

Set or change the passcode

→ Navigate to the Setting application, then click on Touch ID and Passcode
→ Touch Turn On Passcode or Change Passcode
For options to create a passcode, click on the **Passcode Options** button. The safest options are Custom Numeric Codes & Custom Alphanumeric Codes.

Change when your iPad automatically locks

→ Enter the Settings application and touch Display and Brightness
→ Touch Auto-Lock, and then select a duration

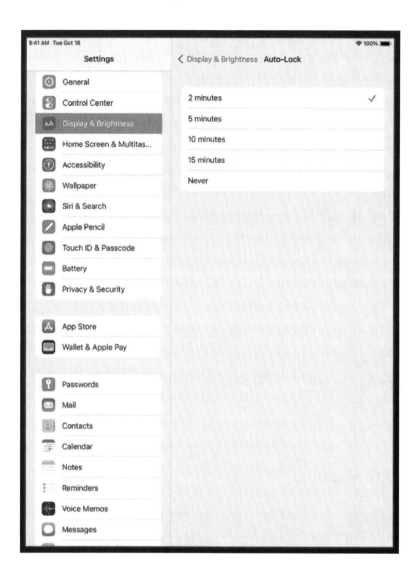

Delete data after ten failed codes entries

Set your device to delete all data, media, & other settings after ten consecutive failed entries.

➔ Navigate to the Setting application, then click on Touch ID and Passcode

➔ Activate Erase Data

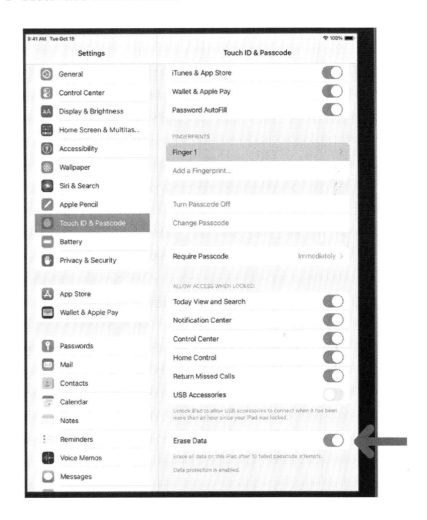

Turn off the passcode

➜ Navigate to the Setting application, then click on Touch ID and Passcode
➜ Touch Turn Off Passcode

Setup Touch ID

With Touch ID, you can easily unlock your device, confirm purchases, and payments & log into a lot of 3rd party applications.

You need to setup a passcode before you can make use of Touch ID.

Enable fingerprint recognition

➜ If you did not setup Touch ID when setting up your iPad, simply enter the Settings application and tap on Touch ID & Passcode.
➜ Activate any of the options, and then adhere to the directives on your display

Add a fingerprint

You can add more than one fingerprint.

➜ Navigate to the Setting application, then click on Touch ID and Passcode

➔ Touch the **Add a Fingerprint** button
➔ Adhere to the directives on your display

Delete or name a fingerprint

➔ Navigate to the Setting application, then click on Touch ID and Passcode
➔ If you've registered more than one fingerprint, place one of the fingers on the top button.
➔ Touch the fingerprint, then give it a name or touch the **Delete Fingerprint** button

Disable Touch ID

Navigate to the Setting application, click on Touch ID and Passcode, and then disable any of the options

CHAPTER 14

UPDATE YOUR IPAD

Your data will not change when you update your device to the latest version of iPadOS.

Before updating your device, setup your device to backup automatically or back it up manually.

Update your iPad automatically

If you did not activate the Automatic Updates feature when setting up your device, do the following:

→ Enter the Settings application, touch General, touch Software Updates, and then touch Automatic Update.
→ Activate Download iPadOS Update & Install iPadOS Update

If there's an update, your device will download the update overnight while it's connected to WiFi & power. You'll receive a notification before your device installs the update.

Update your iPad manually

You can check for & install software updates at any time.

Enter the Settings application, touch General, and then touch Software Updates

Your screen will show the currently installed iPadOS version & if there's an update.

CHAPTER 15

BACKUP & RESTORE

Backup your iPad

You can backup your device using your computer or iCloud.

Use iCloud to back up your device

→ Enter the Settings application, touch [your name], touch iCloud, and then touch iCloud Backup.
→ Activate iCloud Back up
   iCloud will automatically backup your device every day when it's connected to WiFi, charging, & locked.
→ Click on the **Backup Now** button to manually backup your device.

To find your iCloud backups, enter the Settings application, touch [your name], touch iCloud, touch Manage Account Storage, and then touch Backups. To delete any of the backups, select one of the backups from the backup list and then click on the **Delete and Turn Off Back up** button.

Use a Mac to backup your device

➜ Use a cable to connect your iPad to your Mac.
➜ Select your iPad on your Mac's Finder side bar.
➜ Click on the **General** button in the upper part of the Finder window
➜ Select "Backup all data on iPad to Mac."
➜ Select "Encrypt local back up" to encrypt & password-protect your data.
➜ Click on the Backup Now button

Use your Windows PC to backup your device

➜ Use a cable to connect your iPad to your Windows PC.
➜ In the iTune application on your computer, click on the iPad button in the iTune window.
➜ Click on the **Summary** button
➜ In the Backups section, click on the **Backup Now** button.
➜ Select "Encrypt local back up", then click on the Set Password button to encrypt & password protect your data.

To view the backups saved on your PC, select Edit > Preference and then click on the **Devices** button. The password-protected backups have a lock icon in the backup list.

Restore contents from a backup

You can restore your data from a backup to a new or recently erased tablet.

Restore from an iCloud backup

➔ Switch on your new or recently wiped iPad.
➔ Touch the **Setup Manually** option, touch Restore from iCloud Back Up, and then adhere to the directives on your display.

Restore your iPad from a computer back up

➔ Use a USB cable to connect your new or recently wiped iPad to the computer that has the backup.
➔ Carry out any of the below:
  • On your Mac's Finder side bar(macOS 10.150 or after), select your iPad, click on the **Trust** button, then click on the **Restore From Back up** button
  • On a Windows computer or a Mac(macOS 10.140 or before): Launch the iTunes application, click on the iPad button in the upper left part of the iTunes window, click on the **Summary** button, then click on the **Restore Back up** button.

➜ Select one of the backups from the catalog, then click on the **Continue** button

If the backup is protected with a passcode, you'll have to insert the passcode before you can restore your data

CHAPTER 16

SIDECAR

The Sidecar feature allows iPad users to use their device as their Mac's second screen. The Sidecar feature allows you to:

→ Use different applications on the different displays.
→ Use one application on the two screens. For instance, you can preview an artwork on your Mac's display while using your Apple Pencil & an application's tool on your iPad.

→ Mirror the screen so that your iPad & your macOS device show the same thing.

Setup Sidecar

→ Ensure you are using the same Apple ID on the two devices
→ Make use of any of the connections below:
- Wireless: Ensure you have activated WiFi & Bluetooth on your MacOS device, and you have activated Bluetooth & WiFi on your iPad. Both devices have to be within Bluetooth range(33ft)
- USB: Use a USB cable to connect your iPad to your Mac
→ Carry out any of the below on your Mac:
- macOS Ventura: Select Apple menus , click on Systems Setting, click on Display , click on the Add Screen button , then choose your iPad from the list in the **Mirror or Extend to** section
- macOS 10.150 to 12.50: Select Apple menus , click on Systems Preference, click on Display , click on the **Add Display** button, and then choose your iPad from the list in the **Mirror or Extend to** section.

Use Sidecar

→ After connecting your iPad to your Mac, carry out any of the below:

- Move a window between displays by dragging the window or holding the cursor over the green button in the upper-left edge of the window, then select the **Move to** button.
- Use your iPad's side bar: With your Apple Pencil or finger, touch buttons in the side bar to display or conceal the menu bar⬚, the keyboard⬚, or the Dock⬚. Or touch any of the modifiers buttons, like Ctrl∧, to use a shortcut.
- On your tablet, switch from the Mac's desktop to your iPad's Home Screen: To enter your iPad's Home Screen, swipe up from the lower edge of your iPad's display. To go back to your Mac's desktop, touch the Side Car icon ⬚ in your iPad's Dock.
- Mirror the screens or change the screen's layout(macOS Ventura): Select Apple menus , click on Systems Setting, and then click on Display⬚ in the side bar. Scroll down on the right, then click on the **Arrange** button
- Mirror the screens or change the screen's layout(macOS 10.15 to 12.5): Select Apple menus , click on Systems Preference, click on Display⬚, then make the needed adjustments

➔ When you want to stop making use of your iPad, carry out any of the below:

- On your tablet: Click the Disconnects button ⬚ at the lower part of the side bar.
- On your MacOS device: Click on the Controls Centre icon ⬤ in the menu bar, click on the **Display** button, and then unselect your iPad from the list in the **Mirror or Extend to** section.

INDEX

Made in United States
Orlando, FL
28 November 2024

54599241R00124